THE DELINQUENCY LABEL: THE EPIDEMIOLOGY OF JUVENILE DELINQUENCY

THE DELINQUENCY LABEL: THE EPIDEMIOLOGY OF JUVENILE DELINQUENCY

Victor Eisner _{UNIVERSITY OF CALIFORNIA, BERKELEY}

RANDOM HOUSE : NEW YORK

FOR MY CHILDREN

Foreword

Crime throughout the nation has increased to the point that insecurity on our streets and in our homes has been declared one of our foremost national problems. If official records are an adequate index, juvenile delinquency and crime are outracing our capacity to deal with them.

Unhappily, and notwithstanding the earnestness of the effort, control of juvenile delinquency and crime continues to emphasize the traditional measures of arrest, detention, and incarceration. We have yet to assess correctly the consequences of our control measures or their relevance to the processes that are generating the steadily increasing numbers of those we have labeled delinquent.

The public fails to see that they are saddling the police, the courts, and penal correctional facilities with abortive routines— routines so dangerously misconceived and overtaxed as to create the very conditions they are meant to repress. Obviously we must take an entirely new look at the phenomenon of juvenile delinquency. For every delinquent or criminal who commits an overtly hostile and aggressive act there are many more whose latent hostilities keep them from being productive members of society.

The problem of juvenile delinquency continues to be dealt with by social policies that reflect the simplistic assumption that the behavior of a delinquent boy or girl is ipso facto the sign of willful disregard for legitimate authority and hence evidence of a

personal defect and/or shortcoming. We have only begun to ex-
plore the mysteries by which societies unintentionally produce
criminal responses in some of their members; it has become
increasingly apparent that the self-same social structure that produces persons disrespectful of the law also produces conformists.
Quite possibly the behavior that our society notes and deals with
as juvenile delinquency is a normal reaction of normal individuals to an abnormal condition.

The epidemiological methods employed in this study are well
designed to grapple with the vexing issues that are confounding
us in our efforts to control the crime problem.

We continue, too often, to fail in our assumptions, if not in
our rhetoric, when we say that delinquency and crime are the
lengthened shadow of the community. Although the community
is changing drastically, the detailed conditions of the change are
obscure. The epidemiological model may be useful in making
explicit these obscured variables and in bringing to the surface
the latent influences and forces that make the incidence of juvenile delinquency disproportionate for different groups within the
population. At the very least, the model is designed to focus our
attention upon the differential criminogenic impact of our system of juvenile justice as well as upon the influences that operate
to call boys and girls to the attention of that system.

The changing patterns of delinquency and crime are a projec-
tion of far-reaching changes in American community life. The
police, the courts, the machinery of punishment and corrections
are also projections of the community. It is not likely that we
will be successful in controlling juvenile delinquency without
seriously changing the organization and administration of juvenile justice. We must see juvenile delinquency not only as a
problem in law enforcement but also as a problem in education,
family organization, employment opportunity, and housing. It is
inside these structures that deviance and, hence, delinquency
incubate. It is a myth that behavior can be changed directly. It
can be changed only by altering the conditions that enter into
and underlie behavior. We must learn to find and treat causes,
not only effects, of delinquency and crime.

Joseph D. Lohman

Acknowledgments

This book contains both data and opinions. The opinions, of course, are my own. But I could never have collected the data or completed an analysis without help from many people. It is a pleasant task to list their names, for each name recalls hours of discussion as well as specific help.

Two co-workers made essential contributions to my studies. Henry Tsuyemura of Keneoke, Hawaii, worked with me on 1960 statistics. Chapters V and VI report studies in which he shared; the theoretical background of this portion of the analysis owes much to his experience. The analysis that forms the core of Chapter VII and that is described in Appendix B-V was designed and carried out by Harley B. Messinger, M.D., who coauthored these sections of the book. Dr. Messinger selected appropriate techniques, carried them through the necessary computer calculations, and interpreted the results.

I am indebted to Thomas F. Strycula, formerly Chief Juvenile Probation Officer in San Francisco, and to Thomas J. Cahill, Chief of San Francisco Police, for permission to use San Francisco Juvenile Court and Police Department data. The juvenile-court data were provided by Mrs. Ann C. Billyard, Chief Statistician of the Juvenile Court. Police-department data were supplied by Edward Comber, Director of Criminal Information, and by Captain William A. Hanrahan, formerly Director of the Police Juvenile Bureau, and his staff. Mrs. Billyard, Director Comber, and Captain Hanrahan's staff guided me through their files and answered many questions about procedures and records.

San Francisco Health Department data were used with the permission of Ellis D. Sox, M.D., Director of Public Health for the City and County of San Francisco. They were supplied to me by Miss Mildred Holota, Chief of the Health Department's Bureau of Statistics, and by her staff, who may yet forgive me for the disorder I created in their IBM card files.

The Research and Statistics Subcommittee of the San Francisco Committee on Youth, under the chairmanship of Louis Weintraub, coded and punched the IBM cards for individual delinquents. The committee under Mr. Weintraub, in addition to Mrs. Billyard, Director Comber, Miss Holota, and myself, was composed of Daniel A. Collins, Jane H. Fator, Bertis L. Jones, S. C. Kohs, Frank M. Moncrief, and J. M. Rogers. During my terms on this committee I had the advantage of sharing in many discussions of the meaning of delinquency statistics and of the current delinquency picture in the city. I am especially grateful for the education I received from all the committee members. Our discussions often ended in disagreement, but I always learned something from them.

Writing a book requires more than having material to present. I cannot overstate my debt to Feleni B. Little, editor at the University of California School of Public Health. Mrs. Little went over every page of my manuscript. She did more than just excise dangling participles and ambiguous pronouns; her insistence on consistency of style and logical organization converted a difficult, stodgy manuscript into one that I trust reads easily.

The revisions resulting from Mrs. Little's editing were ably handled by Mrs. Lois Miller and Mrs. Mary Hurst, who typed countless drafts of every chapter and who complained only when the manuscript was illegible, not when it was difficult.

I would also like to acknowledge the contributions of Elizabeth Sue Dooley, Berkeley, California; Sigmund Eisner, University of Arizona; and Percy Pinckney, Director of Streetwork, Youth For Service, San Francisco. They read portions of the manuscript and made valuable suggestions.

The quotations in Chapter X from Claude Brown's *Manchild in the Promised Land,* copyright 1965, are used by permission of the Macmillan Company. The quotation from R. Abrahams' *Deep Down in the Jungle,* copyright 1964, is used by permission of Folklore Associates, Inc., and that from Charles Keil's *Urban Blues,* copyright 1966, by permission of the University of Chicago Press.

Throughout the writing of this book my wife, Rosemarie, had to put up with bursts of enthusiasm when she was not putting up with spells of preoccupation. Nevertheless, she gave me her constant and invaluable support, advice and encouragement.

Victor Eisner
Berkeley, California

Contents

THE DELINQUENCY LABEL: THE EPIDEMIOLOGY OF JUVENILE DELINQUENCY

I: THE DELINQUENCY PROBLEM

· 1 · DIMENSIONS OF THE PROBLEM

A prominent cleric recently attributed increasing crime to widespread compassion for "junkies, dope fiends, throat slashers, beatniks, prostitutes, homosexuals, and punks" (*San Francisco Chronicle*, January 28, 1967). The implication is that our "compassion" is preventing adequate punishment of delinquents and that delinquent behavior can be eliminated or sharply reduced by the deterrent effects of severe punishment. He links this concept to a view of deviance that sees so little difference between types of unconventional behavior that a beatnik can be equated with a prostitute and a throat slasher with a homosexual.

This book is written from a different point of view. Delinquents, like other people, act as they do because of events in their past and because of situations in which they live. If our objective is to reduce delinquency, we must understand the reasons why certain juveniles violate the law. As a first step, we should know which groups of youth are most prone to become delinquent and we must learn as much as possible about the environments that produce delinquents.'

Crime and delinquency are certainly closely related. They are not the same, for what constitutes a crime if done by a person over 21, is called a delinquency, and handled by a different administrative mechanism, if done by a person under 18. Many

3 :

acts which are delinquencies if performed by minors are not crimes if done by adults: for example, drinking alcoholic beverages. The exact age at which a juvenile becomes a young adult, and his misdeeds become crimes rather than delinquencies, will be discussed below. Regardless of precise definitions, crime and delinquency are certainly increasing in every major city of the United States, and juveniles and young adults are the source of the greatest danger to law-abiding citizens. Detention facilities are overcrowded. Police forces find themselves the targets of civilian resentment as they try to protect the inhabitants of cities from disorder and lawlessness. Traditional measures to control juvenile delinquency are apparently becoming less and less effective (Chaitin and Dunham, 1966). This situation calls for a new approach to the entire problem. Instead of continuing with methods that have failed in the past, we need to devise new methods based on sound knowledge. Punishment has consistently failed to eliminate antisocial behavior, but so have measures designed to rehabilitate delinquents.

The search for new directions for delinquency control can start in any city of the United States, since all have similar problems. My investigations were carried out in San Francisco and consisted of a series of studies made between 1963 and 1967.

San Francisco, like other cities, had been suffering from ever-increasing numbers of juvenile offenders. By 1960, San Francisco's Juvenile Hall, built to house a maximum of 195 children, had an average daily population of 256 (San Francisco Juvenile Court, 1960). Other facilities for juvenile offenders were similarly strained.

San Francisco had traditionally prided itself on being "the city that knows how." Before 1940 San Franciscans boasted that they had no slums. Although labor strife had been a problem in the 1930s, by World War II the major labor problems had been solved, and civic boosters looked forward to a future of constant progress. But San Francisco proved to be no different from other major cities of the United States. The war and its upheavals, migration, the "flight to the suburbs," freeways, air pollution, and slums all affected it after 1940, just as they did other cities. By 1960 the city faced severe problems. One was juvenile delinquency.

San Francisco made its first attack on delinquency in 1960, when the mayor designated a group of leading citizens as the Committee on Youth. This committee promptly appointed a subcommittee on research and statistics and charged it with the task of developing statistics on juvenile delinquency. My studies, which were made partly as a member of this subcommittee and partly as an independent investigator, originally were designed as an epidemiological analysis of the data collected by the subcommittee. As the work progressed, it became increasingly evident that the major social problems that lead to delinquency overshadowed the problems of individual delinquents.

Juvenile delinquency is not an isolated pattern that can be studied outside of the context of the society in which it occurs. An act of an individual is delinquent only when society, through its laws, has defined it as illegal. Society's role in defining delinquency goes beyond a simple listing of illegal acts, because our law-enforcement mechanism recognizes extenuating circumstances. These circumstances must be considered in order to determine if the youth who has committed a specific illegal act is to be defined as a delinquent. The system we have devised for controlling antisocial behavior of young people provides a wide area in which law-enforcement personnel must make judgments. The application of these judgments affects delinquency statistics. In some cases (to be explained in subsequent chapters), the manner in which we enforce our laws becomes a factor tending to promote antisocial behavior.

The adverse effect of law enforcement on the delinquency of certain groups is not trivial. At the time of the subcommittee's first report, in 1964, arrest rates of Negro boys were so high that it was impossible to consider arrest as a deterrent to delinquency. The high arrest rates actually foreshadowed the race riots that began in San Francisco in 1966. The delinquency statistics, which we shall see later, demonstrate that there are groups of youths who are alienated from our main society. This group alienation has been one of the clearest findings of my studies. Because of its importance, we shall concern ourselves with not only statistical but also nonstatistical illustrations of it —and we shall do so in the case of two of the groups of alienated youth whose problems were studied: lower-class Negro boys in urban ghettoes and middle-class white boys in the suburbs. Both groups are characterized by a large number of delinquents. Lower-class Negro boys show the highest delinquency rates. Delinquency rates for middle-class white boys are low, but the problem of delinquency in this group is greater because there are a larger number of these boys. Both groups live in environments that lend themselves to detailed study. In addition the groups demonstrate two important segments of the delinquency problem, which Lin Tsung-yi (1959), writing about delinquency in Taiwan, called "modern" and "traditional" delinquency. We in America think of the two parts of the problem as the delinquency of youth in the dominant group in our society and as the delinquency of youth who live in an "underground" subculture.

The behavior of adolescents in these two groups shows resemblances at several critical points. The similarities, rather than the differences, between the delinquency of middle-class white boys and of Negro gang boys illustrate the major thesis of this book, which is that juvenile delinquency cannot be equated with deviant behavior. The role of society in producing delinquency is far more important than the role of individual deviance. The delinquent may be, in fact usually is, a normal member of a deviant group rather than a deviant from a normal group. We must look at delinquency in the framework of the social and economic structure of our society; and when we study delinquency, we must be prepared to examine our basic assumptions about the nature of our social system and our methods of child rearing.

My studies lead to the conclusion that the structure of our society forces certain groups of youth into delinquent patterns of life. We have institutional barriers that effectively prevent these youth from abandoning delinquency—and we shall want to identify these barriers. New methods for controlling delinquency must remove them and integrate delinquent youth into the law-abiding portion of the community. Such an achievement requires a change in the delinquent youth, of course, but it also requires a change in the attitudes and institutions of American life.

• 2 • THE EPIDEMIOLOGICAL METHOD

Dr. John Snow, a respected London physician of the first half of the nineteenth century, walked one day into Broad Street in the heart of the slums. He went to the community well, detached the pump handle, and walked away with it under his arm.

At that time cholera was rampant in England. Epidemics broke out, spread, and disappeared without apparent cause, killing men, women, and children who only days before had been in the best of health. Dr. Snow was the man who explained how cholera spread and who established the methods, which we still use, to prevent it. He removed the pump handle because he was convinced that the well was a source of infection; he had conducted an epidemiological investigation (J. Snow, 1855) that showed that the infection was spread by sewage-contaminated water. His investigation had consisted of measuring the risk of cholera in population groups that differed from each other in the type of water they drank.

Dr. Snow started by finding out how long it took an epidemic to travel from place to place. It moved at just about the same speed as people did when they traveled, and he theorized that the disease was transmitted from person to person. Further study led him to believe that it was transmitted by an agent in the body discharges of its victims. As a result, he suspected the water supply. London at that time had two suppliers of piped water; it also had local wells. One water supply was unfiltered and came directly from a place on the Thames where ships anchored. The other, drawn from a point far up the river, was filtered. The two suppliers were in vigorous competition, and both served all areas of London; they even competed for and served houses within a single block.

Dr. Snow discovered that he could distinguish between the two water supplies by adding a little silver nitrate to the water. The unfiltered downstream water, due to its higher salt content, formed a white precipitate with this chemical. Armed with this information, he investigated the water supply of individual houses and obtained from death certificates the addresses of all people who had died from cholera. He found that the risk of dying of cholera was eight times as high for those drinking un-filtered water as for those drinking the filtered supply.

This observation was an epidemiological one that confirmed his theory of the transmission of cholera and led eventually to his trip to the Broad Street pump. His epidemiological studies also led to my studies of juvenile delinquency, which, like his, should help to eliminate the sources of a particular condition. Before describing my work, let me describe my methodology, which was similar to Dr. Snow's.

Epidemiology is a study of relative risks. The epidemiologist estimates the risk of the appearance of a condition in one popu-lation group and compares this risk with that for another group. The risk can be expressed as the proportion of the total popula-tion group who actually get the condition. The estimate of the risk requires counting both the members of the total group and the number who had the condition. In Dr. Snow's case, he counted the people who were served by each water supplier and the number in each group who died of cholera. For study pur-poses, groups may be formulated in various ways: for instance, people of different ages or races or people living in certain areas. If the right groups are chosen, a comparison will show which people are most vulnerable to a particular condition. Finding out why these particular people are so vulnerable should lead to better control methods.

Epidemiological methods are as well adapted to the study of delinquency as to the study of cholera. Juvenile delinquency, despite loose usage of the word, is not an epidemic. It resembles cholera, however, in that it is distributed unevenly throughout the population. Certain groups of people appear to have a high risk of becoming delinquent, just as certain people had a high risk of contracting cholera. But the causes of delinquency are more complex than those of cholera. No germ will ever be re-vealed as the cause of delinquency, and no single "pump handle" can be removed to protect a community from it. Delinquency appears most frequently in areas where there is poverty, adult crime, or a constellation of community values that are grouped under the names of "anomie" or "social disorganization" (Shaw and McKay, 1942; Lander, 1954; Chilton, 1964). The groups that produce delinquents often influence their members to engage in activities that are illegal; members of a street gang support each other in actions that would be unacceptable in a YMCA camp (Cloward and Ohlin, 1960). Individuals are not equally susceptible to these influences; such factors as physical or intellectual capability or the type of family in which they grow up may make the difference between delinquency and conformity (Redl and Wineman, 1951; Kvaraceus, Miller et al., 1959; Glueck and Glueck, 1962). In 1965 S. Rubenfield attempted to reconcile apparent inconsistencies in the vast amount of research on the individual delinquent, his social group, and his community. He pointed out how these forces interact, and showed that neither "sociological" nor "psychological" explanations of delinquency are complete by themselves. Both personality and society are important determinants of behavior.

In the presence of conflicting theories and ineffective control measures it becomes appropriate to look at the populations that produce high rates of delinquency, to describe them as accurately as possible, and to isolate the factors related to the high delinquency rates.

As already indicated, the epidemiological method is basically a comparison of risks for different segments of the population. The risk of delinquency is best expressed as a rate. This can be defined as the number of individuals in a particular classification who become delinquent out of each thousand in the classification. Mathematically, this is a problem of division: Risk equals delinquents divided by population. The result is then multiplied by 1000 to convert it to rate per 1000 at risk. Thus to calculate a risk, we need know only the number of delinquents and the number of people of the same type (called the "population at risk") who might have become delinquent. For example, if the number of delinquent boys in a community who are aged 8–10 and 11–13 is known, and the total number of boys in each of these age groups is also known, risks for each group can be calculated and compared. If there were 2000 boys 11–13 of whom 20 were delinquent, the risk of delinquency for boys at that age would be 10 per thousand. When the population is divided in more complex ways, however (as, for example, by age, sex, and race simultaneously), it may be quite difficult to determine both the numerator and the denominator. A large part of this book will be concerned with the exact methodology used to determine them. The main purpose of the mathematics is to compare risks and to find out which people form high-risk groups.

Although this method sounds simple, it has rarely been used to study delinquency. There have been only two previous epidemiological studies of delinquency. In 1961 J. W. Eaton and K. Polk published a study of the delinquent juveniles of Los Angeles, and in 1963 S. R. Hathaway and E. E. Monachesi, in a study of adolescent personality, related juvenile delinquency in their study population to their entire group of subjects.

Eaton and Polk obtained information about the delinquent population from the Los Angeles County Probation Department. Their data covered all Probation Department referrals for 1956. The population at risk was estimated, as their study year was between censuses. They looked at the effects on delinquency of age, sex, ethnic group, marital status of parents, and geographical mobility. They also studied the nature of the offenses charged against the youths. They showed that delinquency was primarily an adolescent phenomenon that involved boys four times as often as girls. Moreover, whether or not juveniles were members of a minority group was significant. The Negro and Mexican minorities had far higher rates than the white majority. Since the Japanese minority had lower rates than the white majority, however, their findings could not be entirely related to restricted opportunities for minority groups. But other data seemed to offer an explanation: Children from broken homes had an increased risk of delinquency, and broken homes occurred less often in the Japanese population than in any of the other groups. The Eaton and Polk study also showed that recorded rates of recidivism reflected administrative procedure far more than they reflected actual delinquencies. Geographical mobility did not appear to influence delinquency rates to any great extent.

As a result of their study, Eaton and Polk recommended a thorough review of the prevention and treatment of delinquency and also recommended administrative changes in the probation department. They suggested that control measures should be directed at family instability rather than at individual children, and they recommended improved official protective services for children, especially for the five-to-nine age group.

Hathaway and Monachesi studied ninth-grade white children to whom they gave a psychological test, the Minnesota Multiphasic Personality Inventory. They followed them thereafter for three to four years. They divided their population by age, size of community, father's occupation, type of family, and intelligence of the child. They scored delinquency from 0 to 4 depending on the number and severity of recorded offenses. They found that delinquency rates decreased as their subjects reached nineteen years of age. Also, delinquency rates varied inversely with socioeconomic status and were higher for children from broken homes. The rates did not vary with intelligence but did vary inversely with high-school rank. They also varied with population density, but Hathaway and Monachesi related this finding to occupation rather than to community size, as rates were very low for children of farmers. They were unable to develop a delinquency-proneness scale from their data; however, they pointed out certain personality types who were liable to become delinquent.

These two studies provide valuable information, but they do not answer all the questions one might ask. It is not enough to say that Negro youth have high delinquency rates. Negroes are generally poor and poor people also have high rates. They live in areas of high delinquency: This also would be expected to influence the rates.

Take the case of a Negro boy whose father does not live at home. Is he a higher delinquency risk than a white boy of the same age and education, who lives in the same neighborhood, and whose father also does not live at home? This question can be stated in more general terms. Is the correlation of delinquency with race independent of such other factors as income, place of residence, and family structure? That is, does a boy's race have a really important bearing on delinquency, or is it important only that he grow up with certain social and economic advantages? The same sort of question can be asked about each of the other factors associated with high delinquency rates.

The epidemiological method was chosen for my studies in order to answer these questions. In some cases, I found answers. In others, the findings served only to raise new questions.

A word of caution. Epidemiology deals with populations, not with individuals. Membership of an individual in a high-risk population does not necessarily mean that he is extremely liable to become delinquent; it means only that a high proportion of his group will. Analogously, one might say that a high IQ puts a child at "high risk" of getting good grades in school, but some brilliant children may nevertheless get low marks. Even a 70 percent risk of delinquency in a particular population group does not justify treating any member of the group as a delinquent unless he actually becomes one. We shall observe in later chapters the consequences of a policy of treating all members of a group as delinquents.

• 3 • DELINQUENCY LABELING

In September 1966 a policeman shot and killed a sixteen-year-old Negro boy in the Hunters Point section of San Francisco. A riot exploded that afternoon and ended only after the National Guard had been called out.

This explosion was the first "race" riot in San Francisco, and it had an unusual result. Instead of calling for more police in Hunters Point, civic leaders started immediately to locate jobs for unemployed minority-group members. Hundreds of unskilled jobs were advertised during the next few months.

In November fifteen boys who had been enrolled for six to seventeen months in the Neighborhood Youth Corps, a federal job-training program, were taken to apply for one of the new positions that had appeared after the riot. All of them were rejected on the basis that they had police records and were therefore ineligible for bonding. Their experience highlights an important facet of juvenile delinquency.

If their experience were unique it would not be important, but it is a common problem. Boys with police records are virtually unemployable—not because they are minority-group members or because they are unskilled, although both of these are handicaps; not because of lack of education, for high school graduates with police records have the same difficulty. They are unemployable because there are no jobs for delinquents.

This situation leads to a question that must be answered as the first step in a study of delinquency: What is a delinquent? If a study, like this one, consists of counting delinquents, the question is a methodological one. But the question is even more important for people engaged in programs for combating juvenile delinquency, for the answer to "what is a delinquent" will influence the measures used to prevent delinquency and will even determine whether or not it is possible to rehabilitate delinquents.

The usual definition, that a juvenile delinquent is a person under twenty-one years who has violated the law, has important uses in the right places and is necessary, for example, to police and courts. From a practical point of view, however, a delinquent is any person who has been labeled as a delinquent. This definition has its own advantages—not the least of which is its operational logic, which simultaneously explains the experiences of the Neighborhood Youth Corps and validates a study of delinquency based on official records.

Recorded juvenile delinquency is not a direct measure of the amount of lawbreaking by the youth of a community. For this reason various methods have been used for estimating the "true" amount of juvenile delinquency from various types of delinquency statistics. The working definition used in this study directs the investigation to the phenomenon of recorded delinquency itself. The delinquency label is important, and this label should be studied. Two types of activity go into the labeling process: the activities of juveniles and the activities of law-enforcement agencies. A study of the delinquency label must be done through a study of records, because it is primarily the existence of a record in the files of law-enforcement agencies that constitutes the label. The study becomes an examination of interactions between juveniles and law-enforcement agencies.

To illustrate the process of labeling an individual as a delinquent, let us examine the hypothetical case of a teen-age boy involved in a street fight between two groups of adolescents. When he has been picked up by a policeman and his name recorded, three decisions have already been made: first, he has committed an offense; second, the offense warranted intervention; and third, it was necessary to record his name. A further series of decisions, which may be called administrative, follow. The process of recording the event requires that a name be given to the delinquent act. The names from which the choice is made come from the list of actions the community has previously specified as violations of the law. (Appendix A shows the list in use in San Francisco in 1960.) Such lists include a wide variety of actions, from playing ball on the streets to homicide, but in our example the boy might be charged with assault, disorderly conduct, fighting, or curfew violation. When a name has been chosen for the offense, the policeman fills out a card with the juvenile's name, age, offense, and other identifying data. He then must decide whether he should release the juvenile or cite him to juvenile court. If he cites him to juvenile court, the court must make still more decisions. First, there must be an investigation, which determines whether a petition will be filed, making the case an "official" one, or whether it will be handled as an "unofficial" case. Next there are all the steps leading to a decision as to whether the boy will be held in custody, made a ward of the court, placed on probation, or released. J. D. Lohman (1957, p. 17) summed up the labeling process by saying, "It becomes apparent that the description of a child as delinquent is primarily a function of police policy, court standards, and community sentiment."

Several aspects of this labeling process must be emphasized. The first of these is the question of guilt or innocence. At the time of this study, San Francisco juvenile courts were organized to function on a completely different basis than the adult courts. Adult courts are institutions charged with determining a suitable punishment, and conviction in an adult court is the best available proof of guilt. As P. W. Tappan (1947, p. 101) has said, "Adjudicated offenders represent the closest approximation to those who have in fact violated the law, carefully selected by the sieving of the due process of law; no other province of social control attempts to ascertain the breach of norms with such vigor and precision."

This statement was not true of the mechanisms used for dealing with juveniles. Not until May of 1967 did a Supreme Court decision (*in re* Gault *et al.,* 387 U.S. 1 [May 15, 1967]) guarantee juveniles the same constitutional protection that adults have in the adult courts. Until then the juvenile-court philosophy could be expressed in the following quotation from a publication of the United States Children's Bureau (1960, p. 38):

Many people think of a juvenile court as either doing little or nothing with children who break the law or as a place where punishment is meted out. Neither of these views reflect what a juvenile court is supposed to do or how most courts function. Their philosophy is one of individualized justice fitting court action to the child. The juvenile court was founded on the principle that its prime responsibility is to understand, protect, and help the child or youth—not to punish him. This means that the court is more concerned with the delinquent child himself than with his specific offense.

The juvenile court was charged with investigating the circumstances of an alleged offense and taking appropriate action to promote the welfare of the juvenile. Strictly speaking, it did not determine guilt except incidentally to its task of seeking action in the best interest of the juvenile, nor did it administer punishment except for the purpose of rehabilitation. It is a paradox that the mechanism that society had set up to "understand, protect, and help the child or youth" was often the very mechanism that, by labeling him as a delinquent, made him unemployable and thus sentenced him to a life of poverty. The difficulty was, and still is, that once a juvenile appears in juvenile court charged with an offense, his name and alleged offense become a matter of record in many states, even if the case is dismissed. A juvenile can acquire the label of delinquent whether or not he is actually guilty of an offense. This paradoxical situation does not mean that most of the juveniles seen in court were innocent, but it does mean that the court records and records of police contacts that constitute a "police record" and make a youth unemployable may include persons who have not really been guilty of law violations.

The second important aspect of the labeling process is shown by a curious omission. An examination of Appendix A, the list of charges used for juvenile offenders, would lead to the conclusion that the only reason for arresting a juvenile is that he has committed an offense. Another common reason is delinquency prevention (Piliavin and Werthman, 1967). Many of the interactions between juveniles and policemen are due to the desire of the police to prevent more serious offenses. A curfew violation is often recorded, for example, if a policeman believes that a youth may be about to commit a more dangerous offense. Appendix A contains no category called "prevention." The list is composed of offenses against persons, offenses against property, and offenses against community customs or morality. (Some of the group of offenses listed under "delinquent tendencies," such as curfew violations, insubordination, runaway, or possession of liquor, can be considered examples of the last category.) The community has, it is true, passed laws against these activities, but the purpose of many of these laws is to prevent other activities that would actually constitute a danger to the community. A boy who is picked up at 2 A.M. and cited to juvenile court for "delinquent tendencies" has not injured the community. The purpose of the citation is to prevent a serious law violation. Nevertheless, the boy has received a delinquency label.

One more point about the labeling process: There is no way to reverse it. Once the label has been applied, a boy remains either a delinquent or a former delinquent. This consequence is contrary to the original purpose of juvenile courts, but it is unavoidable. The members of the Neighborhood Youth Corps, whose experiences began this section, were trying to start a nondelinquent life. They were as far along the road to rehabilitation as they could travel unless they succeeded in obtaining permanent work. Their enrollment in the Youth Corps and their performance as enrollees had shown their interest in preparing for a job and were evidence of their motivation. If job-training programs could not make them employable, it is hard to see what else they might have done. Their only legal recourse was to have their juvenile-court records sealed. To seal these records is possible, but in California and many other states it does not remove the label. As a matter of fact, it may make the label seem even worse as sealing the record does not make it disappear. All that disappears is the record of the court appearance; the fact that the juvenile appeared in court remains in the files. This may lead one to imagine an offense more serious than the one committed. The boy can deny that he appeared in court only at the risk of prosecution for perjury. This state of affairs remains in effect at the present time, in spite of the Supreme Court decision referred to above, recent changes in the wording of questions on civil service examinations, and federal programs for bonding former delinquents. These measures are alleviating the situation but they have not eliminated it.

The actual labeling is carried out by three law-enforcement agencies, each of which keeps its own records. These agencies are the police department, the juvenile court, and what I have called adult courts: local, state, and federal courts that normally do not have primary jurisdiction over juveniles. The record of an offense by a person under twenty-one may appear in the files of any of these agencies.

In San Francisco, the police department keeps a separate file for records of juvenile offenses. This file has two parts. One consists of an alphabetical card file, arranged by year, and contains the "Incident Cards" filled out by each policeman when he interrogates a juvenile. These cards contain identifying information; the offense or suspected offense; the place, date, and time; and qualifying remarks. Cards for juveniles cited to court are kept separately from cards for juveniles who are "warned but not cited." The other part of the record contains cards, arranged alphabetically, that give for each juvenile the offense and the date of each police contact. These cards constitute a cumulative record of contacts and are used as a source of information on the previous record of the individual.

Juvenile-court records are more elaborate. They include a folder containing the results of an extensive investigation of the offender, as well as the disposition of the case. These records are not permanent; if after several years there are no further entries, they are destroyed. The permanent records contain only identifying data. Thus, when the folder has been removed from the file, much information is lost although the fact that the individual had appeared in court remains in the records.

Adult-court records are pertinent to a study of juvenile offenders because cases involving juveniles from eighteen to twenty-one may be heard in adult courts instead of juvenile courts. Adult-court records were not accessible for this study. They not only are more difficult to obtain, but also are less likely than juvenile-court records to contain hearsay. An adult offender generally has a defense lawyer to represent him and to make sure that he receives all proper protection.

The form and availability of the various types of delinquency records are of importance in designing a study of the delinquency label. Before a recorded delinquency was accepted for use in this study, it had to meet definite, carefully chosen criteria. It seemed that the most useful study would come from counting all individuals between eight and seventeen who had been charged with a nontraffic offense at any time during the study years of 1960 and 1964. The decision to use these criteria was based on answers to three important questions. First, should the record of a police contact be counted as evidence of a delinquency label? Second, what should be counted—individuals or offenses? (For example, if one person had been cited twice to juvenile court, should he be counted in terms of one delinquency label or two?) Finally, what age group should be included in the count?

Police contacts should only be included when counting delinquency if it is a serious matter to appear in police records. A police warning is not a barrier to employment, and offenses for which warnings are given are usually minor. Many of the warnings are given to prevent further delinquency. But each warning enters a permanent cumulative record, and these records certainly increase the likelihood that a new offense will be handled by citation to court. The records constitute a sort of character reference for a juvenile, and when a policeman has had many occasions to "warn" a boy for minor violations, the boy becomes an object of legitimate suspicion when the police are investigating a new incident. In addition, each contact is an interaction between a juvenile and law-enforcement agencies in which only a decision by the policemen is needed for the interaction to end with a court citation rather than a warning. For these reasons police contacts have been included among the interactions that constitute recorded delinquency.

The second question brings in the whole problem of repeated offenses: the study of recidivism. Recidivism is a problem of tremendous social importance but is exceedingly difficult to investigate. The boy who repeatedly violates the law is far more of a danger to the community than the boy who commits only one offense. No one has devised a satisfactory way to study recidivism—for two reasons. First, there is the simple matter of mobility. People do not remain in one place all their lives, and a study of repeated offenses should include all episodes that occur in all places where the person has lived. San Francisco is a small city surrounded by a large number of urban and suburban areas that are within easy reach by public or private transportation. Many San Francisco delinquents have records in other cities in the area. No cross-filing system is available to the police, and to be thorough a study of recidivism would require records from each area in which each boy had lived or visited. Even if an investigator solved this problem, he would encounter another.

This other problem arises from the fact that the status of a juvenile offender affects the way in which a second offense is recorded. In general, if a youth is being processed for a previous offense, a new offense is liable to be recorded as an aggravation of the first one. An example might be a boy who is stopped for a curfew violation but who begins to fight with the policeman. At another level, an example is a theft committed while a boy is on probation. In neither case does a second offense become a part of the record. In the first example the record may show one offense, disturbing the peace. In the second, it will show only a violation of probation. Inconsistencies in the manner of recording multiple offenses are why Eaton and Polk concluded that the statistics on recidivism reflected administrative procedure as much as they reflected the actions of juveniles. They also explain why, to answer the second of our three questions, offenders rather than offenses are counted in the study in this book. Each delinquent is counted only once in a given year, regardless of how many offenses he was charged with; the total represents the number of people who were labeled as delinquents in that year.

The decision of what age group to use was made on two bases. The younger the child, the more likely that officials will consider the offense to be the result of parental neglect. No child under five is held responsible for his actions. As he grows older, society of course considers him increasingly responsible. Because there were only fourteen children of five to seven who were charged with offenses in San Francisco in 1960, it was decided arbitrarily to set a minimum age of eight years.

Cases of persons over seventeen were not included because adult-court records were inaccessible. Juvenile delinquents of eighteen, nineteen, and twenty were found in both the police and juvenile-court records, but together they totaled only a tenth of the number of seventeen-year-olds. The inference is that nearly all the older offenders appeared in adult courts.

These decisions involving police contact, recidivism, and age groups determined the form of this study. A count of all individuals between eight and seventeen who had been charged by the police or juvenile courts with offenses in a given year does not measure the delinquent acts of the juvenile population. It measures the number of the juvenile population whose actions society has decided to restrict in some manner and whom society has labeled as delinquent. The individuals who are counted may or may not have engaged in illegal activities, but they all have been labeled as delinquents.

A minor source of error in the count of interactions between juveniles and the law may come from the possibility that a policeman who questions a juvenile or stops some activity of his may not record his name. In San Francisco this failure to record a name is against police policy, and members of the police department give assurances that the number of such incidents is negligible. Nevertheless, each unrecorded contact was an interaction of a type that would have added depth to the study. To the extent that unrecorded contacts occur, a study of delinquency labels of course falls short of being a study of all interactions.

On the other hand, so-called hidden delinquency is not a source of error for this study. An undetected violation of the law obviously does not result in either an interaction or a label of delinquency. Nor does it result in remedial or punitive action by society. Delinquent acts that do not result in a delinquency label are quite properly left out of the count.

A delinquent has been defined as any person whom society labels as a delinquent. The use of official records to count delinquents implies this definition, and the long-term consequences of a delinquency label support it. In this book recorded delinquency will be used to measure the interactions of juveniles with the law.

II: OBTAINING INFORMA-
TION ABOUT
DELINQUENTS

One evening late in 1960 a policeman surprised a boy, whom I shall call Joseph Torres, in the act of removing a portable radio from the glove compartment of a parked automobile. The police-man knew Joseph by sight as one of a group of boys who were frequently out late at night. He felt that the boy needed a severe lesson and arrested him. He recorded Joseph's name and wrote down that he was Mexican, fourteen years old, 5 feet 6 inches tall, about 130 pounds; had black hair, brown eyes, swarthy skin; and was dressed in black trousers and a yellow jacket. He also filled in Joseph's address (in census tract M-4) and the location of the incident, at 21st and Capp Streets (in census tract N-8). He recorded the offense as "auto boosting."

The next day, in the Youth Guidance Center, juvenile-court investigators began to gather more information about Joseph. They discovered that he lived with his mother, two younger brothers, and a stepfather who had moved into the household six months before. His father had died eight years ago, and his mother had subsequently become an alcoholic. Both parents had been born in Nicaragua, and Joseph had been born in Arizona. Joseph was a Catholic, in the eighth grade of a public junior high school. The family income, from the stepfather's wages and the mother's part-time work, was about $4,000 per year. Joseph had been seen twice before in juvenile court—first, at the age of nine, when a "neglect petition" had been filed, and second, in January of the current year, at which time he had been the youngest of five boys arrested while riding in a stolen automobile. After investigation the case against him had been dismissed.

After this investigation a delinquency petition was filed. Joseph's case was heard in juvenile court, and he was placed on probation.

Joseph Torres was one of 3,243 San Francisco youths between eight and seventeen who were seen in juvenile court in 1960, and one of 5,412 who were labeled as delinquents during the year. His case illustrates the problem to be discussed in this chapter: What information do we have in a study of records, and what information can we use?

We cannot obtain all the information we want about Joseph Torres from a study of juvenile-delinquency records. For example, it may be crucial to our understanding of him to appreciate his feelings toward his stepfather. If so, we shall never understand him, for the records do not give this information. If we want to study why he stole a radio, we must find another way to do so.

The epidemiologic method restricted the scope of the study even further, because much information in Joseph's record could not be used. Each item of information used in this type of study must meet two criteria. First, it must classify the case into one (and only one) division of a meaningful category. For example, if age is a meaningful category (which it is, since delinquency varies with age), the pertinent item of information is that Joseph was fourteen years old. It allows us to say that Joseph belongs in the fourteen-to-sixteen-year division of the age category. It also allows us to say that he does not belong in any other age group. This first criterion did not exclude much information. Most of the data on Joseph's record are meaningful, in that they describe an individual delinquent, and it is not hard to code each item appropriately into categories of information.

The second criterion restricts the study far more. In an epidemiological study of delinquency it must be possible to divide into the same categories not only the delinquent population but also the population at risk. Religion illustrates this point. It is not difficult to determine the divisions of a category of "religion" and classify Joseph as a Catholic, but the category cannot be used. No one knows the number of the population at risk—that is, San Francisco youths—who belong to the various religious groups. The best estimates are only guesses made by each church on the basis of attendance figures. A certain percentage of all delinquents belongs to each religion, but this information does not tell us anything about the relative risk of delinquency.

The necessity of using only information that could also be determined for the population at risk restricted the study to the use of eight categories. These categories are the sex, age, and race of the delinquent himself; the address, income, and composition of his family; and two administrative items: the offense charged against the delinquent and whether or not he was cited to juvenile court. All these items could be ascertained for all the delinquents except family composition and family income, which were available only for court cases. More important, the population at risk could be broken down by sex, age, race, address, income, and family composition, although not by all these at the same time. As a result, it was possible to study the effect of all of these factors on delinquency rates and also to study the effects of certain combinations of factors.

Before discussing the factors used in the study, more should be said on what was left out. I have already mentioned two items: the quality of a delinquent's relationship with his family and his religion. The first is of known importance. The Gluecks (1950) have used it as part of a five-item test of delinquency proneness. This quality of a delinquent's relationship with his family affects the illegal actions of the juvenile only indirectly. It is not known to law-enforcement officials until after the juvenile-court investigation (if, indeed, it is known at all). But if such information were available for the population at risk and for delinquents, I would very much like to include it. The amount and type of adult influence that increases or decreases the risk of a boy's becoming a delinquent is information directly related both to delinquency prevention and to rehabilitation. Even though it does not directly affect the labeling process, it affects the delinquent acts for which a boy is labeled as a delinquent.

In a subsequent chapter, I shall discuss a factor that shares this advantage: the number of parents in the delinquent's home.

The necessity to omit a study of the effects of religion on delinquency is less disturbing. Religion seems to play a minimal part in the formation of the value system of most adolescents, although it is a part of the culture in which they grow up. I believe that indicators of race and social class are better measures of this culture in present-day America than religious affiliation.

Many other pieces of information about Joseph Torres could not be included in the study. His previous offenses were not included, for reasons given in Chapter III. Information on his geographical mobility would have been useful, however, if population data had been available, to find out whether delinquency is a phenomenon of local residents or of immigrants. One frequently hears, "Our boys are all right. It's those kids who came in from so-and-so who don't know how to get along in our city."

But the unused data on Joseph Torres is not the most important omission made necessary by the design of the study. Because the study is of interactions between juveniles and law-enforcement agencies, lack of information about the actions of the police constitutes the most significant omission.

No information is available from official records about the policeman's mental processes while he is deciding how to handle a particular offender. I. Piliavin and S. Briar (1964) have studied the factors that determine whether or not a policeman will consider a juvenile's actions worth investigating. They have shown that the policeman must take into consideration not only what the juvenile is doing at the moment he is observed (usually through the window of a police car) but also such things as dress, demeanor, the time of day or night, the neighborhood, and recent crimes and misdemeanors in the area. These factors are accessible for other types of studies, but not for an epidemiological study of records.

The actual distribution of the police force over the city was also not a matter of record. If there is no policeman on a particular street, a boy can remove a radio from an automobile, as Joseph Torres did, with much less risk of apprehension than if the neighborhood is heavily patrolled. Policemen in patrol cars have a large area to cover, and they tend to spend most of their time where past experience indicates they are most likely to be needed. It is possible to obtain maps of patrol-car areas. In San Francisco a patrol-car area is large, covering several neighborhoods, and although the average number of policemen in such an area can be determined, this does not tell what parts of it are heavily patrolled. Thus, there is no way to estimate mathematically the likelihood that a delinquent act in a given neighborhood will be observed.

Lack of information about police activity put an important restriction on the conclusions of the study. Any observed difference in delinquency rates, with few exceptions, might in theory be due to a difference in the delinquent activities of juveniles, or to a difference in police enforcement of the law, or to a combination of these factors. Nothing in the study can be used to distinguish between these causes.

This restriction should be taken into account in interpreting the items of information about an individual delinquent. Information that was both available and useful fell into six categories: sex, age, race, address, income, and family composition. Sex, race, and age are immediately obvious to a policeman, who can also make some inferences—from dress, speech, and the neighborhood in which the contact is made—about income and the area of the city from which the juvenile comes. Of the six factors, only one is completely unknown to the policeman at the time he first stops a juvenile: the composition of his family. Thus, all but one of these factors may affect delinquency rates because of the influence they have on the actions of the juvenile, on the actions of the policeman, or on both.

San Francisco is a particularly favorable place in which to study the factors of race and geographical location because of its geographical and cultural diversity. It is a combined city and county situated at the tip of the peninsula that forms the southern boundary of the entrance to San Francisco Bay. It occupies an area of only forty-nine square miles, separated from South San Francisco, an industrial area, and the "Peninsula," largely a suburban area, by a range of hills that are crossed by several highways. On the west it is bounded by the Pacific Ocean, and to the north, beyond the Golden Gate Bridge, are the suburbs of Marin County. The eastern shore of the bay contains the urban center of Oakland and a large complex of urban, industrial, and suburban areas known collectively as the East Bay. These areas are connected to San Francisco by another bridge. Thus, San Francisco is the core of a large metropolitan area for which it has remained the business, financial and commercial center. The population of the city proper was 740,316 in 1960; the remainder of the urban complex (that is, the Standard Metropolitan Statistical Area as defined by the U.S. Bureau of the Census, which does not include the contiguous San Jose SMSA, 50 miles to the south) contained 2,043,043 people.

The city is divided geographically by many natural and artificial barriers, including steep hills, large parks, and freeways. They make it a city of many neighborhoods, each with its own distinctive population and physical characteristics. The geographical barriers that separate the neighborhoods also make it easy to identify them, and a San Franciscan will nearly always locate his home by the district he lives in rather than by the name of a street. The boundaries of the census tracts used for subdividing the city in the decennial census also follow the geographical barriers. The census tract in which a person lives is a category that is available for study and that characterizes a fairly homogeneous neighborhood. The larger divisions, the census areas, which in San Francisco are designated alphabetically, nearly all represent well-defined districts of the city.

The population of the city is also unusually cosmopolitan. San Francisco has long been famed for its colorful minority groups: not only the Italian population of North Beach and Fisherman's Wharf and not only Chinatown, one of the largest areas of Chinese population outside of China, but also many groups less visible to tourists. Among white minority groups can be listed a large Mexican population and an equally large group from countries of Central America. There are cultural enclaves of Russians, many of whom arrived after the 1918 revolution, and other Slavic groups. Germans, Basques, Greeks, and others maintain their cultural identities. The largest non-

white groups are formed by the Negroes, who immigrated to
the Bay Area in large numbers starting in 1942, and the Chinese, who first arrived during the nineteenth century, but who are
still entering the city in appreciable numbers. Japanese form a
far smaller group than they did before 1942, but many Japanese
returned to San Francisco after World War II. Filipinos,
Samoans, and others from the Pacific Islands also live there.
American Indians have been entering the city in recent years
as a result of the relocation programs of the Bureau of Indian
Affairs. The cultural diversity of the city is illustrated by a local
radio station, which broadcasts in fifteen languages.

The San Francisco Police Department recognizes four major
racial groups in its records. These groups are white, Negro,
Mexican, and "other." In a strict sense, they are not really
races, as one of them is a nationality, and they do not conform
to the census definitions that can be used for the population at
risk. The juvenile court uses the first three groups, but sub-
divides the "other" group into a more detailed classification.
Their classification is compatible with the police coding, and
therefore it is also different from the census definitions.

This study reclassifies race into five groups: white, white-
Spanish, Negro, Chinese, and other. These particular groups
were selected partly because of the limitations of the data and
partly from a consideration of the reasons a racial category
would be useful in the study. (The exact method used for this
reclassification is described in Appendix B, which contains the
study methodology.)

The reason that race is an important category in a study of
delinquency has nothing to do with biology. No one has ever
been able to show that any biologically defined race behaves
any differently from another if all other factors are equal. Of
course, all other factors are never equal, but racial differences
in behavior are so bound with cultural differences that one is
completely justified in saying that they are entirely due to the
culture. The culture may be one shared by members of a racial
group (Rainwater, 1966) or by members of an economic or
language group (Lewis, 1966), but each culture has its characteristic behavior.

Race is useful as a category in a study partly because racial differences reflect cultural differences. But the classification is useful in another way. Other people may, and usually do, treat members of a particular racial group as if they belonged to the commonest culture of that group. This is part of the general human tendency to try to fit strangers into familiar categories. Because most Negroes belong to the lower social class rather than to the middle class (regardless of how social class is defined), there is a tendency to treat all Negroes as if they belonged to it. For example, a policeman who stops a Negro boy on the street does not know his personal value system or his aspirations, but he does know his skin color. If this particular policeman believes that Negroes are liable to be lawbreakers, he will often treat him as if he were in fact a lawbreaker.

A meaningful classification by race should take into account the groups that perceive themselves as different and those that others perceive as different. Although "Mexican" is not a racial category, it corresponds to a group that law-enforcement agencies believe to have high delinquency rates. Chinese are regarded as having low delinquency rates.

Ideally, a racial classification should include these two groups. Practically, the "Mexican" group presents special difficulties, as it does not correspond to any grouping that could be made for the population at risk. Joseph Torres illustrates the difficulties in the classification. Although Joseph's parents came from Nicaragua and he was born in the United States, the policeman who arrested him wrote down that he was a Mexican (possibly because of his appearance, his name, or the way he talked). Had his skin been darker, he might have been perceived as an Indian and classified into the "other" racial group. In April of that year, when he was counted in the census, he was listed in census tract M-4 as a white, with the additional qualification that he had a Spanish surname.

The grouping "White with Spanish surname" does not correspond to "Mexican." It is a heterogeneous group, which might include anyone from a descendant of one of the Mexican governors of California to a Tarascan Indian. For practical purposes, however, it contains nearly all the Spanish-speaking population of San Francisco. It probably includes all individuals whom a policeman would classify as Mexican and others whom he would call white. It thus became the closest practical approximation of the Spanish-speaking portion of the population. For convenience this group is called "White-Spanish" in this study.

Joseph's case illustrates another problem in classification. When arrested, he was living with his mother and stepfather— that is, with two parents. But placing him in this group does not take into consideration the early death of his father and the long period during which his mother was the only adult in the family. There seemed to be no way to overcome this problem. The only data available for the population at risk were from the census, which gave the number of children living with two parents as of April 1960. The census classified stepparents and adoptive parents with natural parents and did not distinguish between them.

The category of family income is another that presented problems. Here, however, the difficulty was not in deciding what the category should be, but in achieving accuracy. There are two possible sources of error in the classification. One concerns the delinquent population; the other, the population at risk. Fortunately, the errors tend to cancel each other. One error arises when analyzing families in which more than one person earns an income. A juvenile-court investigator probably would not be informed of all sources of income in all such families, although the investigator in Joseph's case may have been. The other error is the result of the census listing of family income by number of families rather than by the number of children in families with a certain income. An estimate of the net effect of these two errors (see Appendix B) is that they resulted in an apparently lower delinquency rate in the lowest income group, but that the error was not large enough to alter the conclusions given in the next chapter.

The remaining categories for the study, those of age and sex, presented no particular difficulties. Both categories could be determined fairly accurately for both the delinquent population and the population at risk.

The story of Joseph Torres has been used to illustrate the process of extracting information from official sources for use in an epidemiological study of delinquency. When completed the process gave these facts about Joseph: white male with a Spanish surname, age fourteen-to-sixteen, living with two parents, family income of $2500–$5000, census tract M-4, appeared in juvenile court in 1960, charged with theft.

III: DELINQUENCY RATES AND THEIR DETERMINANTS

· 1 · HIGH-RISK GROUPS

In an alley in the South of Market district in San Francisco there is a two-story warehouse with peeling paint and a sign, "Youth For Service." Inside, the ceilings have been repaired with egg crates, and several battered desks, tables, and chairs furnish an office. The agency works with delinquent boys on the streets of San Francisco; its operating personnel are known as streetworkers. Youth For Service streetworkers go into all areas of the city, where they make contacts with gangs of adolescent boys and try to help them undertake a variety of nondelinquent activities.

One of the ongoing programs of Youth For Service is known as ABC. These letters stand for "Always Be Cool" and refer to activities designed to reduce tensions between gang boys and policemen. The program has been in operation for several years. Originally it consisted of rules of conduct for boys stopped by a policeman:

1. State *your* name.
2. Give *your* address.
3. Give name of *your* school.
4. Give name of employer (if employed).
5. State where you are going . . . and if asked, where you are coming from.

6. Give your club name . . . if you belong to a club.

7. Be *polite*. Do not act in a smart-alec manner.

8. If you belong to Youth For Service, tell them so . . . *but be polite*, remember.

These hints plus acting in a polite manner, can make a difference. Always Be Cool

In 1966, after long negotiations between the agency and the police department the ABC program moved into a new phase, consisting of lunch meetings between groups of gang boys and police-department leaders. At these meetings, moderated by streetworkers, policemen and gang boys talked to each other to obtain a better idea of each other's complaints and hostile feelings. The meetings were very successful. After the first, the agency director reported its effect to the agency's board. One board member asked if it was planned to have the same boys attend the entire series of meetings. The director answered, "That's what we want to do. We can do it if they're not in jail."

How likely is it that boys in the ABC program will be in jail? Why is it necessary to plan for this contingency since national statistics show that only 4 percent of all children between ten and seventeen are stopped by the police in a year (Perlman, 1963). This section will give the results of the preliminary analysis of the 1960 delinquency data from San Francisco (Eisner and Tsuyemura, 1965). It is indeed very probable that certain groups of San Francisco boys will go to jail. The analysis shows that the ABC program is more relevant to the daily life of these boys than most of the subjects they learn in school. Streetworkers work with "high-risk groups." How high that risk is will become apparent.

As a first step in identifying high-risk groups, separate tabulations were made for boys and girls. Studies for all cities have shown that boys are delinquent far more often than girls. This finding also proved true for San Francisco, where delinquency rates averaged six times as high for boys as for girls. This ratio varied, of course, in different census tracts, but the lowest ratio was 3½ to 1. In one census tract the boys' rate was nine times that of the girls'.

The next primary divisions of the group were by race and by age. The results of these divisions are shown in Table 1. This table shows delinquency rates calculated in the manner explained above. The rates are shown separately for boys and girls in four age groups and for the five racial groups included in the study. They can be interpreted as showing the risk of delinquency for each sex and race at each age.

Table 1: Delinquency Rates (1960) by Sex, Race, and Age*

Interactions	MALES (AGE, IN YEARS)				FEMALES (AGE, IN YEARS)			
	8–10	11–13	14–16	17	8–10	11–13	14–16	17
All interactions								
White	10	47	167	210	1	6	28	27
White-Spanish	18	62	251	444	2	9	36	33
Negro	35	146	381	575	5	39	86	60
Chinese	8	26	54	72	0	1	10	3
Other	3	82	189	310	0	20	54	46
Juvenile court cases								
White	8	33	84	86	0	6	22	10
White-Spanish	13	36	99	173	2	9	31	13
Negro	29	118	252	295	5	37	78	36
Chinese	5	20	40	46	0	1	10	3
Other	2	67	124	184	0	18	49	22

* Numbers of delinquents used in calculating rates are summarized in Appendix C.

Table 1 confirms the fact of different delinquency rates for boys and girls and shows that delinquency varies markedly with age. S. R. Hathaway and E. D. Monachesi had already shown that delinquency rates reached a maximum at eighteen years of age. Because our study went only to seventeen years, we had expected to be unable to show the age at which delinquency began to decrease. No overall decrease appeared for boys; in each of the five races they followed the expected pattern. Male delinquency rates were uniformly highest at seventeen years of age. But girls showed maximum rates at fourteen to sixteen years, with lower rates at seventeen. The difference suggests an interesting parallel with physiological patterns of adolescence. Girls mature more rapidly than boys, and a rule of thumb is that adolescent girls appear about as mature as boys two to three years older. This difference can be seen in dating customs; girls generally prefer to go out with boys two to three years older, and boys generally prefer girls who are younger. The age difference extends to the assumption by adolescents of such adult functions as marriage and childbearing. It also appears to extend to delinquency.

The results so far have identified two of the factors that define high risk: male sex, and age (for boys) around seventeen years. Another factor is apparent in Table 1: The risk of delinquency varies markedly with race. There was adequate reason to assume that we would find this. J. W. Eaton and K. Polk, for example, showed differences between Japanese, white, Mexican, and Negro groups. These differences were paralleled in our studies. We found the lowest delinquency rates for both boys and girls among Chinese, a fact that was true at all ages except for the very youngest boys (eight to ten years old). In order of increasing delinquency rates, the racial breakdown showed a progression from Chinese to white, "other," white-Spanish, and Negro. The highest rates for both sexes at all ages were for Negroes.

This preliminary tabulation indicates that race is an important characteristic in the definition of high-risk groups. The highest risk group is Negro, with rates about 2½ to 3½ times as high as the average white rates, and 4 to 8 times as high as the average Chinese rates. Seventeen-year-old Negro boys, in fact, had an average delinquency rate of 575 per 1000, that is; over half were either warned by the police or sent to juvenile court in the course of a year. The rate of juvenile-court citation for this group was 295 per 1000; the chance of an *average* seventeen-year-old Negro boy going before juvenile court was nearly one in three.

Three factors—income, number of parents in the home, and geographical area—were not included in Table 1 and require separate analysis. The first two presented two methodological difficulties: They were not available in the records of all delinquents, because they were recorded only for juvenile-court cases, and they could not be tabulated by age because of the way they were listed in census data. In the preliminary phase we attempted only to see whether they were factors that were important in the definition of high-risk groups and that could be subjected to more detailed analysis. The number of parents proved to be such a factor and is discussed further in section 4 of this chapter. Family income, however, appeared to be a variable requiring compensation in other analyses, because delinquency varied with income, but in a way that could not be handled with simple techniques.

Table 2 shows juvenile-court delinquency rates by race, sex, and family income. Contrary to our expectation, the highest delinquency rates did not appear in the lowest income groups, except for Negro girls. Girls of all the other races, and white, white-Spanish and "other" boys, showed maximum rates at income levels between $2500 and $5000. The highest delinquency rates for Negro and Chinese boys were in the $5000–$10,000 income group.

Table 2: Juvenile Court Delinquency Rates (1960) by Sex, Race, and Income

| | MALES | | | | FEMALES | | | |
Race	0–$2,500	$2,500–5,000	$5,000–10,000	Over $10,000	0–$2,500	$2,500–5,000	$5,000–10,000	Over $10,000
White	20	70	20	3	8	19	3	0
White-Spanish	18	62	11	2	9	13	3	0
Negro	81	104	121	3	30	22	9	0
Chinese	3	11	14	2	0	2	2	0
Other	6	63	21	0	12	18	4	0

It is difficult to make a general statement about these results except to say that delinquency does vary with income. Possible errors in recording income, both for the delinquent population and for the population at risk, must also be considered in interpreting this table. As explained in Chapter IV and documented in Appendix B, these errors do not seem big enough to cause the large differences observed between the lowest and the next-to-lowest income groups: That is, the finding of maximum delinquency in middle-income groups seems acceptable. But this finding was not completely consistent; it needs confirmation from a study that has more complete income data derived from the population at risk.

Because our data showed that the effect of income was an important one but did not permit us to draw any conclusions with great confidence, it was decided to handle differences in income by making allowances for their effects on other comparisons. Two methods could be used. One was to compare delinquency rates of groups of approximately equal income; the other was to compare rates of groups of unequal income and then to estimate the error that might have been caused by income inequalities. Both of these methods were used for comparisons which will be reported in subsequent chapters.

The number of parents in a delinquent's home did not present the same difficulties. Table 3 shows a preliminary tabulation of this factor. Like Table 2, this table is for juvenile-court cases only and is broken down by sex and race. The presence of two parents in the home is associated with low delinquency rates. In general, the highest rates are found when there is only one parent; there are exceptions in the case of Chinese girls and "other" girls, but the pattern seems clear. Juveniles who have no parents in their homes, have rates slightly above those for juveniles with both parents.

Table 3: Juvenile Court Delinquency Rates (1960) by Sex, Race, and Number of Parents in Home

Number of Parents	MALES			FEMALES		
	2	1	0	2	1	0
White	20	65	23	3	18	10
White-Spanish	19	64	28	5	15	6
Negro	44	100	47	11	31	14
Chinese	9	15	22	1	3	0
Other	27	34	35	10	9	14

These results, like the preliminary results of the racial breakdown, require more study because they do not include all the pertinent information. The data concerning number of parents suffers mainly from lack of an age breakdown for children, although income differences are also important. (Young chil-

·dren are more likely to live with both parents than are older children. Thus older children not only have higher delinquency rates but also are more likely to come from broken families.) A more detailed analysis will be made below. For the present, the preliminary results are sufficient to show that the numbers of parents in the home is also a factor that affects delinquency labeling.

The last of the three factors we are discussing is the geographical location of the juvenile's home. This factor is particularly important to an interpretation of the racial breakdown shown in Table 1, because the racial differences in that table are due partly to peculiarities of the population distribution of the city. The white population included in Table 1 represents every San Francisco census area, all social classes from the highest to the lowest, and districts both with extremely low delinquency rates and with high rates. None of the other groups has such a diverse background. For example, Chinese live mainly in census area A, where Chinatown is a well-known area of low income which was declared a "poverty area" in 1964 by the Office of Economic Opportunity. Negroes live mainly in two large ghettos in census areas J and L, and one integrated middle-class community in area O. Very few Negroes live in the remaining middle-class neighborhoods of the city.

Unlike the factors of income and number of parents, geographical area could be determined for the entire delinquent population and could be examined simultaneously with sex, age, and race. To show the effects of place of residence most clearly, Table 4 gives delinquency rates only for seventeen-year-olds and limits the comparison to areas in which at least one hundred juveniles of a given sex and race were living. Because Chinese would appear in only one census area of the table, they have been omitted. "Other" races are not included because none of the various areas in which they live contain populations of predominantly one race.

Table 4 shows the situation that made the ABC program relevant to the daily life of certain adolescents. In high-delinquency areas, over a third of the white and white-Spanish seventeen-year-olds were recorded as delinquent in 1960. In area

N, the Mission District, which is the heart of the Spanish-speaking community and a low-income residential and commercial district, three-fifths of the white-Spanish boys were stopped by at least one policeman. Only two of the six areas in which large numbers of Negroes live showed rates below 500 per 1000; two other areas showed rates of 711 and 744.

Table 4: Delinquency Rates for Seventeen-Year-Olds by Sex and Census Area (All Interactions, 1960)

Census Area	MALES			FEMALES		
	White	White-Spanish	Negro	White	White-Spanish	Negro
A	246	—*	—	34	—	—
B	185	—	—	6	—	—
C	14	—	—	0	—	—
D	315	—	—	48	—	—
E	245	—	—	15	—	—
F	—	—	—	—	—	—
G	390	—	—	32	—	—
H	395	—	—	0	—	—
I	—	—	—	—	—	—
J	249	360	711	24	49	69
K	429	300	217	103	0	0
L	340	333	409	38	38	51
M	296	377	639	28	21	0
N	337	607	500	58	49	0
O	212	188	744	25	75	66
P	207	—	—	14	—	—
Q	300	—	—	6	—	—
R	0	—	—	0	—	—

* Dashes indicate census area with fewer than 100 juveniles in the category specified.

Obviously, it is useful for members of street gangs to know how to act when they are stopped by a policeman. In some areas this happens to nearly three-fourths of all seventeen-year-old Negro boys. Interrogation by a policeman is a part of the day-to-day life of these boys.

The finding that three-fourths of a high-risk group are delinquent raises another question. Are these boys a danger to the safety of the community, to the property of the community, or to its morals? A study of records does not answer the question directly, but it does allow an answer based on the perceptions of law-enforcement officials. The average delinquency rate for seventeen-year-old Negro boys shown in Table 1 was 575 per 1000. The rate for these boys in juvenile court was 295. Thus, the police had decided that only 51 percent, or about half the delinquents, had committed an offense severe enough to warrant court action. The other half were labeled as delinquent, but released by policemen with a warning.

Table 5 shows the offenses that were charged against delinquent boys. These offenses have been listed in eight categories, each representing the most serious offense charged against the juvenile at any time during the year. The combined categories of assault, robbery, burglary, auto theft, and other theft made up only 21 percent of the total. Unlike less serious offenses, the rates for all except auto theft were lower at age seventeen than at fourteen to sixteen. The commonest charge was "delinquent tendencies." (Curfew violations comprised approximately 90 percent of this category.) This charge was the most serious one made against 65 percent of the seventeen-year-old boys. The conclusion is inescapable: the police did not find most of the recorded delinquents committing acts that were a major threat to the community.

Threats of a different kind are implicit in these figures, however: the threat of a division of the city's population into mutually antagonistic groups and, in the long run, the threat of civil strife. Conflict did in fact break out in 1966, as already noted, when Negroes in the Hunters Point District (which is a part of census area L) rioted against the police. Since that time, similar civil uprisings have occurred in many other cities. This threat inspired the ABC program and other measures; these measures will be described later.

The division of the city into opposing camps is implicit in the delinquency rates shown in Table 4. By no stretch of the imagination can interrogation by the police be considered a friendly encounter. Regardless of a youth's guilt or innocence, the interactions that constitute recorded delinquency are not only hostile encounters, but encounters that engender ever greater hostility. It is doubtful if these interactions serve to deter boys

Table 5: Male Delinquency Rates (1960) by Sex, Age, and Most Severe Offense Charged During Year*

Offense	RATES, BY AGE				PERCENTAGE OF ALL OFFENSES AT GIVEN AGE			
	8–10	11–13	14–16	17	8–10	11–13	14–16	17
Robbery	0	1	3	2	—	1.7	1.6	0.8
Assault	0	3	7	7	—	5.0	3.6	2.7
Burglary	1	7	12	10	8.4	11.7	6.2	3.9
Theft (except auto)	4	12	20	16	33.3	20.0	10.4	6.2
Auto theft	0	2	18	19	—	3.3	9.3	7.5
Sex offenses	0	1	3	5	—	1.7	1.6	2.0
Delinquent tendencies and curfew violations	4	25	109	166	33.3	41.6	56.4	65.1
All others	3	9	21	30	25.0	15.0	10.9	11.8

* Rates below 0.5 per thousand are given as 0. Rates for narcotics violations, homicide, and forgery were all below 0.5 per thousand and are omitted from the tabulation.

from further delinquency, and I believe that the hostility these encounters create has exactly the opposite effect. This would not matter if the interactions were between law-enforcement agencies and only a few deviant members of the community. The statistic quoted at the beginning of this chapter, that only 4 percent of youth aged ten to seventeen are stopped by policemen in a year, is misleading. The community is composed of many identifiable groups, and, when the high-risk groups have been identified, it is no longer possible to say that only a few youths are delinquent. In high-risk groups most youth are delinquent. In our cities the highest-risk group is now Negro boys, and the rates for this group are appallingly high.

The delinquency rates of high-risk groups are sufficient, I believe, to force a complete reevaluation of the usual concept that delinquents are deviants—that is, that they differ in their attributes from the "normal" boys of the community. If 3 out of 4 seventeen-year-old Negro boys in two large districts of San Francisco are recorded as delinquent in the course of a year, I submit that the deviant in this group is the one boy in four who does not become delinquent. But if delinquency is not due to deviant members of the group, one is driven to the conclusion that the entire group, at least by police standards, must live a life that is opposed by the rest of the community. We should speak of deviant groups, not deviant individuals. The delinquent in this group is the normal member of his society. Psychotherapy will not cure his delinquency, and a cure of delinquency will not help him to get along in his society—indeed, it may very well alienate him from his friends and associates.

The police are not to blame for this situation, nor are they happy about it. The standards they enforce are not police standards, but the standards of our society. But if the delinquency rates we have seen are to be blamed on "society," one must go farther and ask who constitutes the society. Whose standards are being violated by Negro boys? Laws are written and police are directed by the voting majority of the community, composed largely of middle-class whites. It is the standards of this group which are being violated, and if the standards are such that a substantial portion of the community cannot adhere to them, it is the middle-class white group rather than the group of delinquents who are to be blamed. The National Advisory Committee on Civil Disorders (1968, p. 10) concluded that "white racism is essentially responsible for the explosive mixture which has been accumulating in our cities since the end of World War II." The delinquency rates we have seen suggest the same conclusion.

One example may clarify this. The laws and customs of the community governing activities in the streets are based on the concept that a street is for the purpose of moving from one place to another. Many of the high-delinquency groups consider the street as an appropriate place for social activities such as meeting friends. Members of such groups are badly handicapped in their normal activities if they are prevented from using the street in this way. The laws and regulations governing the use of the streets are only one element in the network of middle-class customs which are enforced against deviant groups. The sum total of the network is causing the alienation of deviant groups and thus is contributing to civil disorder.

The ABC program is useful, but it does not go far enough. It does not reduce the basic conflict between the majority, with its middle-class standards, and the deviant groups in our society. A program to reduce tension might well be aimed at this middle-class majority, not at the boys and the police.

• 2 • THE EFFECT OF RACE

If I toss a coin 100 times, I expect to get "heads" about 50 times. If I do not get this result, the coin may be loaded. How many "heads" must I get before I begin to distrust the coin? The answer is a statistical one, which requires a "significance test." I shall conclude that the coin is loaded if "heads" comes up a significantly greater number of times than I expect. If it comes up 98 times out of 100, for example, I am sure that the coin is loaded. If it comes up 51 times, I cannot be sure. The significance test tells whether the result is within chance limits (as is a 51:49 ratio) or so unlikely to occur by chance that I must look for some other reason.

Of course, any result *might* occur by chance, including the improbable one of 98 "heads" and 2 "tails." But if the result is as unlikely as 1 to 20, statisticians generally agree to call it significant; and if it is as unlikely as 1 to 100, it can be called "highly significant." A result of 60 "heads" out of 100 tosses is a significant difference from the expectation of 50:50, and this result could be accepted as evidence that the coin is loaded. A highly significant result such as 65 "heads" could be accepted with even more confidence.

A significance test tells only that the observed result is not due to chance and therefore must be due to something else. It does not tell what that "something" is. Was my coin loaded, or did I toss it unfairly? Because statistics do not tell which explanation is correct, common sense and knowledge of the conditions of the experiment must be used. I can conclude that I had a loaded coin only if I know that I tossed it properly.

The appropriate use of a significance test is to test a hypothesis. This test is done by an experiment set up so that the hypothesis is rejected if the results are significantly different from what is expected. This chapter provides a test of the hypothesis that racial differences in delinquency rates are due to the interacting effects of age, income, family structure, and geographical area.

This hypothesis is an important one for delinquency-control programs. It has been argued that racial differences in delinquency rates (as demonstrated in section 1) are due to socioeconomic conditions. These differences exist, as revealed by investigations of every type, including the epidemiological investigation of J. W. Eaton and K. Polk (1961). The reason for questioning the meaning of these differences is that, compared to whites, Negroes are a socially and economically disadvantaged group that has high delinquency characteristics in every factor included in this study except age distribution. The eight-to-seventeen-year population of Negro juveniles contains a smaller proportion of adolescents and a higher proportion of younger children than do the other racial groups. But Negroes live in high-delinquency slums, Negro families are generally poor, and Negro children are more likely than other children to come from families in which there is only one parent. The question is whether these factors are sufficient to explain the high Negro delinquency rates, or whether there is in addition a real racial factor. The answer will determine whether it is sufficient to combat Negro delinquency by improving the economic conditions of Negro families, bringing Negroes out of the slums, and supporting a more stable family life. Such measures might be expected to lower Negro delinquency rates, but if race is an independent factor, they will not be enough, and we must look farther for an answer to the problem.

Racial differences in delinquency do not refer only to Negro-white differences. In addition to high rates among Negroes, the high rates of the white-Spanish group need an explanation. The low rates of Chinese are as puzzling as the high rates of Negroes. Fortunately, San Francisco's cosmopolitan population provides an excellent opportunity to study the effects of race among all these groups.

I started to study racial differences by comparing the delinquency rates for white and white-Spanish juveniles. The white-Spanish group is the closest approximation I could make to the group perceived by the San Francisco police as Mexican. The comparison can be used to estimate the effect that the police view of delinquency rates has on the rates themselves. Chapter III showed that labeling a boy as a delinquent makes him unemployable and thus leads to further delinquency. This labeling is an example of a self-fulfilling prophecy. In the same way, the effect of known high-delinquency rates for certain races may also act as a self-fulfilling prophecy. For example, because studies have shown that Mexicans are a high-delinquency group, the police are justified in predicting that areas with large numbers of Mexicans will continue to be high-delinquency areas and that it is highly probable that Mexicans in these areas will commit delinquent acts. For this reason, they deploy their forces so as to give these areas greater coverage than others. In other words, Mexicans are under closer surveillance than people with low delinquency rates. But the increased coverage will lead to continuing high rates, if only because it is more likely that a delinquent act will be detected when more policemen are nearby.

The continued high rates then become the justification for continued close surveillance of Mexicans.

It can probably be taken for granted that police beliefs about members of different groups have some effect on delinquency rates. The question really is whether the effect is an important one, large enough to cause a major increase in the rates. In 1960, San Francisco authorities little doubted that "Mexicans" were a high-delinquency group. If the effect turns out to be small for the white-Spanish group, it is probably small for other groups as well.

White and white-Spanish delinquency rates were compared by using the data already presented in section 1. Table 4 gives delinquency rates by geographic area. The white-Spanish population is concentrated in six of the sixteen census areas, whereas the white population is found in all of them. If the two races are compared in the six areas where both live, it can be seen that white-Spanish rates for seventeen-year-old boys are higher than the white rates in only three of the areas. They are lower in the other three. Area N is the only one of the six areas where the discrepancy is great; in this area the white-Spanish rate was 607 compared to a white rate of 337. This area is the geographical heart of the Spanish-speaking community, although there are actually more white boys with Spanish surnames living in Area M.

Because the median income in area N is $1200 lower for white Spanish families than for white families, the high rates for white-Spanish juveniles may depend on income differences more than on race. This possibility can be examined in Table 2, which shows the analysis of rates by income for juvenile-court cases. This comparison shows that white-Spanish delinquency rates are lower than the white at each level of income. Poor white-Spanish children are no more delinquent than poor white children, but there are more of them.

The next set of comparisons was made by a method designed to equalize the effects of geographic area, age, income, and family structure. In this method a mathematical technique was used that makes allowances for the geographical distribution of the two population groups. This technique consists of examining the different racial groups only in areas where each race was represented in sufficient numbers and of "adjusting" for census area. An "area-adjusted" rate is obtained by pretending in turn that each area is inhabited entirely by one race and by calculating, under such circumstances, how many delinquents would have come from the area. The results from each area are then added, and the sum is divided by the number at risk to obtain the hypothetical "adjusted rate." In effect, the procedure cancels out the differences due to geographical area: The remaining differences are due to other factors. These hypothetical rates are given in Table 6, which contains only juvenile-court cases, and the adjusted rates are shown by age, income, and number of parents in the family. Table 6 compares three races—white, white-Spanish, and Negro—as the areas studied (J through O) all contained adequate numbers of each of these races.

In Table 6, the differences between the white and white-Spanish group disappear. When the area-adjusted rates are compared by age, only the seventeen-year-old white-Spanish boys and the eleven-to-seventeen-year-old girls show rates that are any higher than the white groups. When they are compared by income, the rates for white-Spanish boys are actually lower than the rates for white boys. They are also lower for girls, except for those with family incomes above $5000; in this instance the white-Spanish rate is slightly higher. The comparison by number of parents in the home also favors the white-Spanish group.

It is difficult to avoid the conclusion that the differences between the groups are the result of socioeconomic factors. White and white-Spanish juveniles who live in the same area under the same socioeconomic conditions do not appear to differ in delinquency rates! The white-Spanish group had higher rates in Table 4 because the comparison did not equalize socioeconomic factors. Apparently, the expectation by the police of high rates among Mexicans did not cause a major increase in the rates for white-Spanish juveniles. We can regard the effect of police expectations as minimal and as an unimportant cause of racial differences in delinquency rates.

Table 6: Area-Adjusted Juvenile Court Delinquency Rates by Age, Income, and Number of Parents in Home

Individuals	AGE				INCOME				PARENTS IN HOME		
	8–10	11–13	14–16	17	0–$2,500	$2,500–$5,000	$5,000–$10,000	Over $10,000	2	1	0
Males											
White	13	45	91	108	27	80	15	3	21	74	25
White-Spanish	11	27	80	165	22	50	8	3	15	55	27
Negro	38	111	267	315	77	111	35	4	47	110	46
Females											
White	2	8	22	20	7	25	2	0	4	26	10
White-Spanish	2	10	37	25	7	13	3	0	4	18	6
Negro	5	30	75	36	27	20	9	0	9	29	14

Table 6 still shows differences between races, however. The manipulation that equalized the effect of geographical area and allowed comparisons by age, income, and family structure resulted in no detectable differences between the white and white-Spanish groups, but every comparison in the table except that for girls in families of $2500–$5000 income shows that the rates for Negroes were higher than the comparable rates for white or white-Spanish people. The discrepancy is not small: In general, the Negro rates are 1½ to 3 times as high.

Discussions of Negro delinquency frequently produce more heat than light. The reason is that the position of Negroes in our society has become a political question that arouses strong emotions. The emotional nature of the question is shown by the frequent use of such imprecise and semantically loaded terms as "right and wrong," "justice," and "respect for law and order."

High delinquency rates among Negroes can be interpreted in many ways, running the gamut between two extreme views. At one end of the scale is the view that the high rates show conclusively that Negroes violate laws more often than do other groups. This view may lead to a conclusion involving the concept of racial inferiority. At the other end of the scale is the view that Negroes do not actually violate the law more often than do other groups. Police discrimination is given as the reason for the high rates, and the conclusion may well be that the white population is overtly conspiring against Negroes.

In my opinion the police are not engaged in a conspiracy against Negroes, and most policemen are dissatisfied with their inability to give Negroes adequate protection against violence and property loss. Nevertheless, they believe Negroes commit more offenses than other members of the community, and therefore they often do things that are regarded by Negroes as acts of discrimination or persecution (Piliavin and Werthman, 1967), even when they are trying to be impartial. At the same time, unfortunately, many Negroes hold attitudes and values that often bring them into conflict with the police, and this conflict is reflected in high arrest rates.

Chapter IV will discuss the conflict between Negroes and police in greater detail. At the present time we need only recognize that the interpretation of Negro delinquency rates is controversial. Before entering the controversy, we shall examine the evidence that we have concerning the rates themselves. This chapter will limit itself to the question of whether race can be considered as an independent factor influencing delinquency rates. The comparison in Table 6 strongly suggests that it can be, at least for Negroes. The final step in the procedure was to test this conclusion by still another method, which took into account all the delinquents, not only those seen in juvenile court. It consisted of equalizing the effects of geographic area and age simultaneously and estimating the effects of income and family structure.

A "comparison area" was selected that was composed of census tracts whose population was mixed white and Negro. For this comparison I included white-Spanish in the white group—a procedure justified by the previous comparison that failed to show a difference between these groups. (Actually, the white population of this comparison area was 89 percent "Caucasian" and only 11 percent white-Spanish. The exact method used to select these census tracts is given in Appendix B, and population data for the area are in Appendix C.) In these racially integrated census tracts, one can assume that the effects of geography are the same for both Negroes and whites. Appropriate allowances were then made for the age distribution of the Negro and white populations by adjusting for age in the same manner as area was adjusted for in the previous comparison. The age-adjusted rates for boys are shown in Table 7, in which rates are shown for each major offense category and a total for all offenses.

This comparison shows a tremendous racial difference in delinquency rates. Total Negro rates are twice as high as the total white rates. This difference is highly significant. Not only are the totals higher, but there are highly significant differences for each offense category except auto theft and sex offenses. After allowance for age differences, the rate for assault and robbery is five times as high for Negro boys as for white boys

Table 7: Age-Adjusted Male Delinquency Rates in Negro-White Comparison Area

Offense	Negro	White
Assault and robbery	20	4*
Burglary and theft	50	20*
Auto theft	9	9
Sex offenses	2	1
Delinquent tendencies and curfew violations	76	47*
All others	25	15*
Total	182	96*

* Highly significant difference between Negro and white rates.

living in the same area. The rate of burglary and theft is 2½ times as high. The rate for curfew violations and "delinquent tendencies" is over 1½ times as high. These are not only statistically significant differences but also large and important ones.

It remains to be shown that the differences are not due to income and to family structure. Even living in the same area, Negro families are more likely than white families to be poor, and Negro children are more likely than white children to be living with one parent. To estimate the effect of these differences on the comparison, it was assumed that the citywide rates by income and number of parents (given in section 1) would hold true in the comparison area. A calculation showed that the factors of income and family structure could each be expected to account for about a 20 percent increase of Negro rates over white. This increase is not enough to account for the differences in rates shown in Table 7, because all of the significant differences were greater than 40 percent and the difference in the total delinquency rates was 100 percent. This comparison indicates that a part of the Negro-white difference is indeed due to socioeconomic factors. Nevertheless, another part, and not a small one, is due to the independent factor of race.

An examination of Chinese delinquency rates reinforced this conclusion. A Chinese-white comparison area was selected in the same manner as the Negro-white area, and the same procedures were carried out. This comparison is shown in Table

8. In this area, the effects of income and family structure were in opposite directions. Although Chinese families were not as likely to have high incomes as white families in this area, the Chinese children nearly all lived with both parents. In balance, the income difference appeared to weigh more heavily, and the expectation was that the Chinese rates should be slightly higher than the white.

Table 8: Age-Adjusted Male Delinquency Rates in Chinese-White Comparison Area

Offense	Chinese	White
Assault and robbery	1	4
Burglary and theft	10	8
Auto theft	7	5
Sex offenses	2	1
Delinquent tendencies and curfew violations	16	32*
All others	3	10
Total	39	60*

* Significant difference between Chinese and white rates..

Actually, the Chinese rates were lower. This would have been a better comparison area if it were larger. There were only seven small census tracts that could be used in it, and there were only forty-four Chinese delinquents and thirty-seven white delinquents in the entire area. Nevertheless, both the total delinquency rates and the rates for "delinquent tendencies and curfew violations" were significantly lower for Chinese than for white boys. This fact confirms the independent nature of racial differences that I found in the Negro-white comparison.

The finding that racial differences in delinquency rates cannot be attributed entirely to socioeconomic conditions is an important one for the high-delinquency Negro population. It implies that Negroes would continue to have higher delinquency rates than whites, even if they were to rise to the same socioeconomic level. And Chinese boys would continue to have lower rates. Nor can this finding be attributed solely to police expectations. True, policemen expect Negroes to commit violations of the law, and they expect Chinese boys to be law-abiding. They also expect Mexican boys to have high rates, as

they do in Los Angeles (Eaton and Polk, 1961). But this
expectation seems to make at best only a small difference. It
is necessary to find another explanation of racial differences.

I believe that the missing element is a cultural one. But
before this matter is considered in detail, we shall look at
findings that bear on the number of parents in a child's home
and the factors that characterize high-delinquency areas. Cultural factors that produce high delinquency rates among Negroes
will be discussed further in Chapter IV. Now we shall take a
look at the remainder of the experimental data, much of which
also bears on the problem of racial differences in delinquency
rates.

• 3 • ANALYSIS OF HIGH-RISK AREAS*

In 1960, census tract R-1, in the extreme southwestern corner
of San Francisco, was the only tract in the city with no recorded
juvenile delinquency. During the year not a single one of the
339 juveniles who lived there, not even one of the 28 high-
risk fifteen-to-seventeen-year-old boys, had a recorded contact
with the police.

Tract R-1 is small. Much of it consists of a shallow lake,
fringed with reeds and harboring flocks of wild birds. Around
the lake are parkland and golf courses. On the north side of the
lake is the inhabited portion, a circular area about a quarter-mile
in diameter, surrounded by highways. This portion is built up in
the usual San Francisco style, with neatly painted row houses
of which 93 percent were built after 1950. The houses average
5.7 rooms per family and are all in good condition. There are
no stores and no commercial activity of any kind. The families
living in this urban island average over $10,000 in income, 89
percent own their houses, and over half of the adults have attended college. If you drive through the curving streets, you
notice that every house is built over a two-car garage. You see
no pedestrians.

* This section was written in collaboration with Harley B. Messinger, M.D.,
Research Statistician at the School of Public Health, University of California at
Berkeley.

For a sharp contrast nearby, you can drive a few miles north and east to the Fillmore District, where three out of four seventeen-year-old Negro boys are labeled as delinquents during the course of a year. On Webster Street in census tract J-8, you will see prostitutes in short skirts and neat blouses who swing large black handbags and eye passing cars. Children are everywhere. Small knots of men gather around parked automobiles or stand in front of pool halls and barber shops. Some people are wearing new clothes; others, old. Some are neatly dressed; others are in tatters. In a typical census tract such as J-8 the homes are old: Many were built before the 1906 fire. There are many pastel concrete housing projects and redevelopment areas of weed-grown empty lots. The housing projects are almost the only new home construction since 1950. Only 3 percent of the families in this area own their own homes, and the average apartment has 2.2 rooms. Only 73 percent of the housing is sound, but the automobiles are shiny, and many of them are new. The median income in J-8 is $3,500 and only 40 percent of the adults have finished high school. In 1960, the population of this tract was 60 percent Negro.

The well-known association of high delinquency rates with slums has been confirmed by many investigations. The reason has never been completely determined, and perhaps never will be. Is delinquency really higher in slums, or is this an artifact of arrest rates? If delinquency is really higher, what is it in the slum that makes it a high-delinquency area?

Most juveniles are delinquent at some time or in some way. At one time or another nearly every growing child will commit an infraction of the law, even if it is nothing more than playing ball on the street (see Appendix A) or stealing an apple from a grocery store. But some children are protected from a delinquency label. Their parents may make restitution for damage or overlook the misdeed because "he is really a good boy." Many children who have broken laws are treated by doctors and psychiatrists, or referred to school guidance counselors, or handled by any of the community facilities that deal with children. Other children are less well protected or less fortunate and find themselves labeled as delinquents. The lower his social status, the greater a child's chance of being labeled as a delinquent for a given infraction, and delinquency labeling is probably at a maximum in an area of high crime and delinquency rates where police activity is concentrated.

Research findings do not support the contention that lower-class children commit illegal acts more often than do middle-class children. Although A. J. Reiss and A. L. Rhodes (1961) showed that self-reported delinquency in a group of twelve-to-sixteen-year-old white school boys was higher among the lower-class members of their study group, other authors (Nye, Short, and Olsen, 1958; Akers, 1964), have found no social class differences in similar groups.

But there is more than research to back the impression that delinquency is common in slums. Crimes against persons and property occur with greater frequency in slums than in middle-class areas. Even though many of these crimes are committed by adults (and thus reported crimes cannot be used to quantify the amount of juvenile delinquency), antisocial acts of juveniles are a feature of slum life. Many slum areas are well known as places where pedestrians are liable to be beaten and robbed. Gang warfare is a slum phenomenon, and so is teen-age prostitution. Perhaps the discrepancy in research reports is due to the fact that the study populations are boys who are in school and do not include those who have dropped out. Perhaps it is due to the selection of populations that contain mainly white boys, and perhaps the areas under study do not include a wide enough selection of slums and prosperous neighborhoods. At any rate it seems most probable that the high delinquency rates of slums reflect not only high rates of apprehension of offenders, but also a real phenomenon of serious delinquency.

The study reported here does not provide a conclusive answer to this question, as recorded delinquency was investigated rather than delinquency itself. Whether or not delinquent acts are commoner in slums than in economically advantaged areas, however, it is a fact that delinquency labels are far more common. City governments have found it necessary to concentrate most of their organized effort to control juvenile behavior in poverty areas, and juveniles living in these areas are the most likely to be arrested.

An investigation of the characteristics of slum neighborhoods requires a very elaborate statistical analysis, because so many characteristics of slums need to be studied. There are three main types of analysis, all of which require computers to handle the extensive calculations. The methods are all similar in that they deal with correlations rather than with risks.

A correlation is a relationship that tells nothing about causation. The amount of rainfall during the summer and the amount of gasoline needed for a power lawn mower are correlated: if either is high, it can be predicted that the other will also be high. In this case, it is obvious that a high gasoline consumption does not cause heavy rains. But heavy rains can start a series of events that eventually require more gasoline to be used in the lawn mower. Unfortunately, nothing in the mathematical relationship between rainfall and gasoline shows which is the cause and which the effect. If it is argued that the lawn mower is a rainmaking machine, the error is in the theoretical concept and not in the statistics.

The various indices that can be used to characterize a slum area—such as income, or the percentage of dilapidated houses, or the delinquency rate—are all correlated with each other. The methods used to study these correlations cannot show which are causes and which are effects any more than they can prove that the lawn mower does not cause rain. Nevertheless, much can be learned by analyzing the relationships of a group of indices. All three of the common methods of analysis have been used to study delinquency.

The first method is called "partial correlations." In this method, the correlation of the variables (that is, sets of indices) with each other is partitioned in such a way that the final result expresses the independent effect of each variable on delinquency. Thus the partial correlation of income with delinquency is the way delinquency would vary with income (or income would vary with delinquency) if all the other variables remained constant.

The second method, "multiple regression," is a predicting device. A mathematical expression is computed that predicts the delinquency rate from the best possible combination of the other variables. It is assumed that the variables that best predict delinquency are the most important factors causing it. This assumption, of course, is not necessarily true, but it can be useful if it is supported by good reasoning. An example of a multiple regression would be the prediction of a wheat crop from such variables as rainfall, sunlight, type of soil, and so forth. A mathematical equation can be derived such that the amount of each variable could be entered into the equation and the equation solved for the expected crop.

The third method is a "factor analysis." This groups the original sets of variables into a much smaller number of "factors." Each factor is composed of the original variables with a weighting or "factor loading" assigned to each variable. (The factor loading is a number that indicates how important the variable is in the factor.) It is then possible to see how delinquency rates are related to each of the factors and to examine each factor to see the factor loadings of the original variables. Each factor can be visualized as a sort of average of the indices included in it. The factor is selected so that these indices correlate with each other to as great an extent as possible.

These methods were initially applied with great optimism to the study of delinquency, but they have not fulfilled their early promise—partly because the methods are basically a study of correlations and therefore show only relationships, not causation. A second limitation is that each measure of a variable in a census tract is an average of many individual measures. If 40 percent of the people in the tract live in dilapidated houses, 60 percent do not. The delinquents may come from the 40 percent or the 60 percent or (more probably) from both. If delinquency is high in areas with many dilapidated houses, one may assume that the risk of delinquency is higher for a boy living in a dilapidated house. One might as justifiably assume that the dilapidated neighborhood has an effect that increases the risk of delinquency for all boys who live in it. Even if there were theoretical reasons for believing that dilapidated housing causes high delinquency rates, the mechanism of the causation would remain obscure until further studies showed whether the delinquents actually came from the dilapidated houses.

Thus area analyses of delinquency rates are subject to important limitations, inherent in the methods themselves. An area analysis cannot show whether the environment causes delinquency (although this assumption is frequently made), nor can it show whether those juveniles who are actually living under certain environmental conditions are the ones who become delinquent. But the analysis can be used to show the precise relationship of delinquency to certain environmental characteristics (such as housing), and it can show the relationship of these characteristics to each other.

The first area analysis of delinquency rates was made in Chicago (Shaw and McKay, 1942). These researchers demonstrated that delinquency rates were high in areas of population change, poor housing, and poverty. Along with high delinquency rates, these areas also showed high rates of tuberculosis, adult crime, and mental disorders.

B. Lander (1954) published the earliest of the studies that used computers for a multivariate analysis. He was able to show that two indices—the proportion of owner-occupied dwelling units and the proportion of nonwhites living in the area—could be used to predict much of the variance of delinquency rates in Baltimore in 1940. He postulated that community disorganization and lack of norms for conduct were the major causes of delinquency.

D. J. Bordua (1959), in a study conducted in Detroit, added "education" and "overcrowding" to the list of variables that could be used to predict delinquency. Instead of "nonwhite" he found that the proportion of "foreign-born" was a significant predictor. R. J. Chilton (1964) in Indianapolis found, however—when he used the same indices that Bordua had used —that only two, "owner-occupied" and "overcrowding" were necessary to predict delinquency rates in that city.

Chilton investigated further by recomputing the Baltimore and Detroit studies and by adding other indices. He also used a factor-analysis method on data for all three cities. His conclusions for the three cities need not be given in detail: Briefly, despite the differences in predictor variables in the three studies, the relationships of the various indices to each other and to delinquency were remarkably constant. The predictor variables were different in the three studies because they were so closely correlated with each other that the choice of one made unnecessary the use of another similar one in the prediction.

Chilton concluded that all of the studies related delinquency to transiency, poor housing, and economic indices. The inherent limitations of the studies led him to another, equally important conclusion. This conclusion (p. 83) was that "questions concerning the relation of delinquency to the degree of organization of an area or to the degree of agreement on norms cannot be adequately answered with delinquency area data and procedures."

This conclusion of Chilton's was the starting point of our studies. We decided to use an area analysis to answer the question of whether the variation of social and economic conditions we could measure in census tracts was sufficient to predict the delinquency rates in those tracts, or whether we could find evidence that would confirm the conclusion reached in Chapter VI: that racial differences in delinquency rates are not due entirely to socioeconomic conditions. The methods used and the results are described in detail in Appendices B and D. In section 2 of this chapter the socioeconomic influences that could be tested included income and family structure; the remaining influences had to be grouped as the effect of "geographic area." Our area analysis also included "income" and family structure (expressed as "nuclear family" index and a "separation" index). In addition we included a health factor ("prematurity" rates) and eight other characteristics: "unemployment," "working women," "occupation," "education," "home ownership," "crowding," "dilapidated housing," and "racial integration."

Our area analysis was run in two parts. The first was an analysis of delinquency rates and area indices in all of the San Francisco census tracts that had a fairly large juvenile population. The second part was an analysis of white, Negro, and

Chinese tracts. We calculated delinquency rates and area indices for the white population in tracts where many white juveniles lived, and for the nonwhite population in tracts where many nonwhite juveniles lived. We called tracts "Chinese" if the nonwhite population was predominantly Chinese, and "Negro" if it was predominantly Negro. If no single nonwhite race was predominant in a tract, we excluded that tract from study. If large populations of white and nonwhite juveniles lived in the same tract, the tract was used once for its white and once for its nonwhite population. Because no data were used twice, the apparent duplication does not matter. The single-race data analysis enabled us to base our conclusions on a mathematical separation of the city into hypothetical areas inhabited entirely by single races.

There were 96 tracts in which we calculated indices for the entire population of the tract. These will be referred to as the "combined data." The second part of the analysis, which will be called "single-race data," contained 109 tracts, of which 75 were white, 22 Negro, and 12 Chinese.

The first results of the two area analyses are shown in Figures 1 and 2. These two diagrams show the results of a factor analysis of the various indices as they appear with their correlation patterns plotted on the surface of a sphere. The Roman numerals I, II, and III indicate the coordinates of each of three mathematically derived "factors" that are composed of a cluster of indices. Factor I contains as its important elements "income," "unemployment," "occupation," and "housing," as well as some other indices all of which are obviously related to economic conditions. Factor III includes "nuclear family" and "prematurity." It probably represents conditions within families that are obviously more difficult to express as numerical indices. Factor II, which proved not to be related closely to delinquency, contains "home ownership" and "working women."

On the diagram, the closer an index (for example, "education") is to the numeral representing the factor, the more important it is to that factor. The closer any two indices are to each other, the higher is their correlation. Thus, Figure 1, which presents the combined data, shows that low income (LOINC)

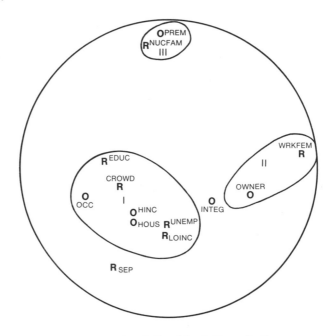

Figure 1. Factor Analysis of Combined Data. Indices appear as if plotted on the surface of a sphere. Roman numerals indicate the coordinates of factors described in the text. The closer an index is to the factor coordinates, the more important it is to that factor. The closer any two indices are to each other, the more highly correlated they are with each other.

and unemployment (UNEMP) are highly correlated with each other and both are in Factor I.

These two diagrams illustrate what the numerical results of the analysis in Appendix D prove: The differences between the two factor analyses are minor. The socioeconomic indices we chose are related to each other in the same way in the single-race data as in the combined data.

The next step was to compute a formula that would use the factors to predict delinquency rates. When this was done, delinquency was best predicted, in both analyses, by using factors I and III. Male delinquency rates could be predicted better than female. Both male and female rates were far better pre-

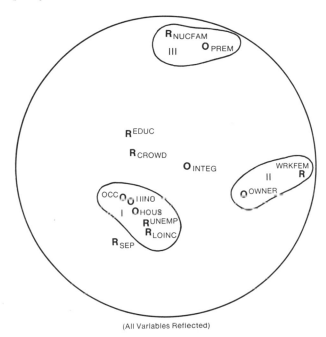

(All Variables Reflected)

Figure 2. Factor Analysis of Single-Race Data. Notice close resemblance to Figure 1.

dicted by using the factors from single-race data to predict rates for each race separately than by using the combined data.

We found four major elements that are necessary to predict delinquency rates in a census tract. One is sex, because male and female rates are quite different. Sex is a trivial element in predicting total delinquency, because it is only under exceptional circumstances that a noninstitutionalized population departs far from a normal sex ratio.

The second element is race. The prediction of delinquency was improved greatly by the use of single-race tracts and could probably be improved even more in our data by adding an arbitrary factor to show whether a tract was Negro, white, or Chinese. The racial effect is a combination of the actions of juveniles and the actions of police and might be expected to vary from community to community. It includes the question of whether police treat members of different races differently: In San Francisco, I believe, police discrimination does not play a large role in racial differences. The effect of race also depends on subcultural differences in behavior.

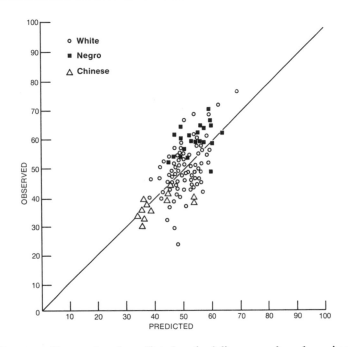

Figure 3. Observed and predicted male delinquency based on single-race data. Rates are expressed as "standardized rates" with a mean of 50 and a standard deviation of 10.

The third and fourth elements in the prediction are those elements that have been identified in the analysis as Factor I and Factor III. As explained above, the elements composing Factor I can be interpreted as economic conditions, and Factor III as intrafamilial conditions. Thus the analysis shows so far that socioeconomic conditions are closely related to delinquency rates. These results are not unexpected, and they confirm the results of other investigators. But there was one more finding from our analysis, a systematic difference by race, that must be considered of great importance. On the whole, the single-race data analysis gave a good prediction of delinquency rates. The prediction was for low rates in the Chinese tracts, where they actually were low, and for high rates in Negro tracts, where they were in fact high. However, the actual rates in Chinese tracts were even lower than predicted, and the actual rates in Negro tracts were even higher than predicted. The differences proved to be highly significant for both boys and girls. This finding is shown in Figures 3 and 4.

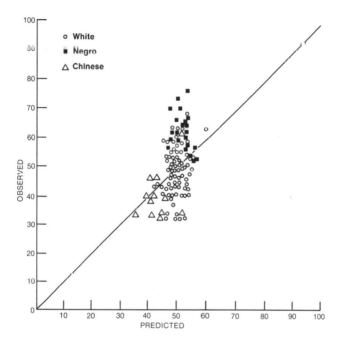

Figure 4. Observed and predicted female delinquency based on single-race data. Rates are expressed as "standardized rates" with a mean of 50 and a standard deviation of 10.

We interpreted this finding as confirmation of the conclusion reached in section 2. Socioeconomic conditions only partially explain the racial differences in delinquency rates. Reasons have already been given for believing that the racial differences are due to something more than the effect of policemen believing that Negroes are a higher-delinquency group; the results of the area analysis again seem to indicate that there is a difference between Negro and white subcultures that accounts for high delinquency rates among Negroes.

With the information we now have about the relationship of delinquency to socioeconomic conditions, we can now consider the question posed earlier in this chapter: What in the slum makes it a high-delinquency area?

On the whole, the rates of recorded delinquency in a census tract are very well explained by social and economic factors. We now know, however, that certain groups of people have higher delinquency rates than the extent of their social and economic problems would indicate, and we also know that other groups have lower ones. It appears reasonable to postulate that this would be true if we had the means for investigating further for other population groups. For example, if we had data to determine average indices for such groups as Mexicans or Filipinos, or for groups characterized by social class, we might well find that delinquency in these groups, too, cannot be completely explained by indices derived from the census tracts in which they live. Our finding is best explained by concluding that the high delinquency rates of slums exist because people with certain types of behavior are liable to be poor and therefore live in slums. To a great extent the slum does not cause the delinquency, it is merely the place where delinquents are found.

When causative implications are read into the relationships of slum conditions and delinquency, one begins to wonder why there can be delinquency when none of these conditions occur. If delinquency were caused by poverty, overcrowding, poor education, or illegitimacy, why would delinquency be high in a middle-class suburb where none of these exist? The answer is that these are coincidental relationships. Poverty does not cause delinquency, but the type of family that is liable to have delinquent children is also liable to be poor.

Chapters IV and V will discuss some of the conditions that I believe lead to delinquency. At this point we shall go no farther than to summarize the results of the area analysis in this way: It confirmed the association of high rates of delinquency with low socioeconomic conditions, but clearly showed that socioeconomic conditions were insufficient to explain all the variations in delinquency rates. In order to explain these variations, one must look at the differences in behavior that characterize racial groups.

• 4 • THE EFFECT OF FAMILY STRUCTURE

In 1939, nobody objected when thousands of children were evacuated from London and sent to foster homes in the country. World War II had broken out. Bombers were expected over the city, and almost everyone believed that children should not remain. Not all of the children were evacuated. The next year, when bombs began to fall, many were still in London, where they slept with their parents in air-raid shelters, even though most people felt that good parents would not expose their children to such dangers.

Now, a generation later, few would agree. The evacuated children constituted an involuntary experiment in mental health, and the experiment turned out disastrously. Many of the evacuated children developed emotional disorders and behavior disturbances; many became uncontrollable and delinquent. The children who remained with their parents adjusted well, despite the danger.

After the war, John Bowlby (1952), in a book that has become a classic, stated a principle that has dominated child care ever since: Children need parents. Bowlby studied maternal deprivation, especially the fate of infants deprived of mothers and placed in institutions and orphanages. He concluded that even a poor home was better than the usual child-care institution. Infants who did not receive maternal love and warmth grew up with severe intellectual and character disorders. Many failed to thrive, some even died.

Bowlby's work was a major influence in changing thought from a "genetic" view of character and personality to a view in which the effects of environment were paramount. Since he published his work, orphanages have given way to foster homes, hospitals have shortened the time that infants have been kept away from home, and working mothers have been encouraged to give up their jobs to remain home with their children. Disorders of all sorts are now blamed on an improper home environment. These disorders include behavior problems, like delinquency, that once were believed to arise from inherent, constitutional factors.

Bowlby himself considered that some delinquency could be attributed to maternal deprivation. This was the delinquency of children with "affectionless characters"—a personality disorder which Bowlby observed in some children who had been raised in institutions. But the environmental situation that is usually blamed for boys becoming delinquent is the home without a father (Glueck and Glueck, 1950; Kvaraceus, *et al.,* 1959). A high proportion of delinquents do, in fact, come from families where there has been a divorce, a separation, or, less often, a death. Adolescent boys need a role model, so goes the reasoning (Bordua, 1960), and if they have no adult male at home to serve as one, they have difficulty in forming a proper masculine self-image. They have more than the usual doubts about their masculinity, which in our culture means their strength, boldness, daring, or fighting ability. To prove their masculinity to them-selves and to their peers, they are prone to engage in activities that demonstrate these qualities. These activities are frequently delinquent.

The evidence for this line of reasoning comes not only from delinquency statistics (Eaton and Polk, 1961; Hathaway and Monachesi, 1963) but from psychoanalytic studies (Witmer, 1960) and appears incontrovertible. All investigations, includ-ing the preliminary analysis of my own data (as reported in section 1), have associated an absent father with an increased risk of delinquency. Nevertheless, when I made a more detailed analysis of this data, I obtained a contrary result (Eisner, 1966). The result has never been confirmed, but it is capable of logical interpretation, and it raises serious questions about our present concepts of delinquency.

Even though all previous epidemiological studies have shown that children without fathers have a high risk of delinquency, these studies are not without flaws. The flaws come from that ever-present problem, the definition of the population at risk.

How many children live with both parents? The answer is readily accessible in published census reports, but it is misleading. These reports tell how many children under eighteen live with both parents. This figure, which is based on a 25 percent sample, is accurate. The difficulty is that it does not tell how many children *of an age to become delinquents* live with both parents. Most delinquents are teen-agers, and more small children than teen-agers live with both parents.

If this problem can be solved, there remains the problem of independence of factors that has already been discussed. Because the loss of a parent means a loss of income, families with one parent tend to be poorer than families with two. Negro children frequently live with only one parent: Are their high delinquency rates the result of family structure, or is this only coincidental? Interrelated factors must be analyzed before family structure can be established as an independent factor affecting delinquency.

In my study of records the number of parents with whom a delinquent lives was the only factor from which conclusions could be drawn concerning the actual delinquent activities of juveniles. Age, sex, race, and to some extent even income and the general area in which one lives can be ascertained by a policeman on sight. Because they are known to the policeman, they may affect delinquency rates in one of two ways. They may influence the actions of the juvenile himself. Age, for instance, certainly does: The illegal actions that an eleven-year-old can think of and that he will actually commit are not the same as those of a seventeen-year-old. Moreover, boys do not act like girls, and poor people do not act like rich people. On the other hand, each of these factors can influence both the perceptions and the actions of a policeman as he makes the series of decisions that eventually lead to delinquency labeling. For example, a policeman in a squad car is less likely to stop a well-dressed Chinese boy walking on a middle-class residential street at night than a poorly dressed Negro boy wearing dark glasses, walking in a neighborhood of low-rent houses dotted with small stores. A fighting ten-year-old boy is less likely to be arrested than a fighting eighteen-year-old boy. Many more subtle factors influence a policeman's decision.

But one cannot tell, simply by looking at a boy, whether his father lives at home. This information is routinely obtained only in juvenile court; the policeman who makes the arrest rarely has it. It is unlikely that the effect of this factor on delinquency rates would be to alter the actions of the police. The effect must therefore be due primarily to its influence on the actions of the juvenile. In other words, children who live with one parent are arrested more often than those who live with two parents because they commit more violations of the law, and not because policemen prefer to arrest such children.

To determine whether the high delinquency rates of children in one-parent families were in fact due to the one-parent factor or whether they were coincidental and due to interacting factors, a method was used that was designed to equalize simultaneously sex, race, age, income, and geographical area. The first step was to obtain better estimates for the population at risk than could be found in published census reports. The estimates were made with data from computer tapes that became available several years after the census was taken (U.S. Census 1:1000 Sample). These tapes included data on a small sample of all children in urban areas in the Western United States with a population of 500,000 or over, and gave a tabulation by color, age, and number of parents. There seemed no way to obtain data for San Francisco only, but I believe that the tabulations obtained from the census tape (Appendix C) allowed a reasonable estimate to be made for the population under study.

The next step was to allow for the effects of income. All the census tracts in the city were grouped according to the median income of the families living in each tract. The tracts were divided into four groups, each containing one-quarter of all the tracts. This step also made some allowance for the effects of socioeconomic factors in different geographical areas: it was assumed at this point that each income quartile represented a division that incorporated both kinds of effect.

The final step was to compute age-adjusted delinquency rates by number of parents in the home and by income quartiles and to perform significance tests on the results. Table 9 shows the results obtained from calculations based on the 1641 white boys and 353 white girls who appeared in juvenile court during the study year.

Table 9: Age-Adjusted Juvenile Court Delinquency Rates for White Juveniles by Income Quartile of Census Tract of Residence, Sex, and Number of Parents in the Home*

Income Quartile	PARENTS IN HOME, MALE		PARENTS IN HOME, FEMALE	
	2	0–1	2	0–1
1 (lowest)	113	124	16	31†
2	69	133†	12	40†
3	48	104†	10	22†
4 (highest)	43	83†	3	16†

* Table is based on 1,641 male and 353 female delinquents.
† Highly significant difference.

Results were just what might have been expected. Delinquency rates for both sexes were higher in all income quartiles in homes with only one (or no) parents. All the differences were highly significant except those for boys in the lowest-income quartile.

Different results appeared when the same calculations were made for nonwhites. These results appear in Table 10, which is based on 979 boys and 270 girls. In this table, boys in the lowest income quartile showed just the opposite effect of family struc-ture; that is, there were more delinquents in two-parent than in

Table 10: Age-Adjusted Juvenile Court Delinquency Rates for Nonwhite Juveniles of All Races by Income Quartile of Census Tract of Residence, Sex, and Number of Parents in the Home*

Income Quartile	PARENTS IN HOME, MALE		PARENTS IN HOME, FEMALE	
	2	0–1	2	0–1
1 (lowest)	147	108†	37	36
2	82	114‡	21	24
3	48	107†	10	34†
4 (highest)	65	45	2	26

* Table is based on 979 male and 270 female delinquents.
† Highly significant difference.
‡ Significant difference.

one-parent or no-parent homes. The difference was significant, and fairly large: in this nonwhite lowest-income quartile boys were a third more likely to be delinquent when both parents were living at home.

This unexpected finding demanded further study. The independent effect of family structure seemed to be confirmed for whites (because it appeared after ·allowance for other factors); among nonwhites, however, it seemed to be more complex than had at first been anticipated. It was possible to study this finding by looking more closely at the factor of race, using a method similar to that used in Chapter VI. The method consisted in examining nonwhite delinquency rates in areas in which there was at least 80 percent of one race in the nonwhite population. As before, a Negro area and a Chinese area could be selected on this basis. Because there was no need to make a comparison with the white population, it was not necessary to restrict the areas to racially integrated census tracts. This allowed use of a Negro area of fifteen census tracts and a Chinese area of twelve. The Chinese area was not large enough, however, to permit an examination of delinquency rates for girls.

As nearly all the nonwhite areas were low-income, a new division into income quartiles allowed a closer look at income factors. This closer look was possible because census tracts that were in the lowest quartile for the entire city proved to be in the second or even in the third income quartile when only the nonwhite areas were included.

Table 11 gives the results of the new tabulations. All calculations were performed in the same manner as for Tables 9 and 10. The results from the Chinese area show the expected pattern: Delinquency rates are lower when there are two parents in the home. The unexpected higher rates with two parents in the home are associated with Negro-inhabited census tracts and therefore appear to be a Negro rather than a white or Chinese pattern. This pattern is demonstrable only in the second quartile: The third quartile showed the expected results, and differences in the first and fourth quartiles were not significant. Thus, the effect of parents in the home is not completely independent of income.

Table 11: Age-Adjusted Juvenile Court Delinquency Rates for Nonwhite Juveniles in Negro and Chinese Areas by Income Quartile of Census Tract of Residence, Sex, and Number of Parents in the Home*

Income Quartile	PARENTS IN HOME, NEGRO MALE		PARENTS IN HOME, NEGRO FEMALE		PARENTS IN HOME, CHINESE MALE	
	2	0–1	2	0–1	2	0–1
1 (lowest)	123	111	39	58	16	34
2	246	111†	35	29	24	59
3	60	105‡	21	28	16	29
4 (highest)	132	117	32	36	16	175‡

* Table is based on 587 Negro male, 145 Negro female, and 44 Chinese male delinquents.
† Highly significant difference.
‡ Significant difference.

When a completely unexpected experimental result is obtained, it is a fair question to ask if it can be believed. Until it has been confirmed by an independent observation, it should remain open to question. These findings are therefore not conclusive on the effect of family structure on delinquency rates. The results reported in this chapter were obtained by indirect methods involving a long series of estimates and assumptions. Even the basic data, the number of parents in a home, may be incorrectly reported to census-takers and to court investigators. The data did not permit the use of a simple method: The census tabulations were not made in a way that would permit them to be cross-tabulated for all relevant factors simultaneously. A study in a school, where information could be obtained for the entire population of delinquents and nondelinquents, might be used to confirm these results, and other experimental designs are conceivable. Until a new experiment confirms this one, any conclusions from this part of the study have to be tentative.

The results are not unbelievable, however. The role of a father in the ordinary Negro household is quite different from that of a father in a middle-class white household. Not only is a Negro father's role different, but the difference has been in evidence for centuries and probably can be attributed to the conditions under which Negroes first came to America. The role is not that of the "head of the house," it often is that of a dependent (Abrahams, 1964; U.S. Department of Labor, 1965).

Unlike most immigrants to the United States, Negroes did not come voluntarily and were not allowed to form families. Those who became economically independent found (unlike white transportees and bondsmen who also came to America in a condition of servitude) that they were excluded from full participation in the normal life of the community (Frazier, 1948). Negro families were deliberately broken up even before the slave ships arrived at American ports. Negro women were treated as breeding stock, and men were used for impregnation of women without being allowed responsibility in the rearing of children. The pattern of family life that resulted was the simplest one possible, short of anarchy: A family consisted of a mother and her children. From this developed a new, matriarchal society of families consisting of grandmothers, mothers, and children. (Technically, this is the wrong term. Anthropologists call these families "female-based." The term matriarchal is used because it is more familiar to most readers.) This pattern has persisted into the present time and is readily visible to observers in the Negro ghettoes of all of our cities (Rainwater, 1966).

In this type of matriarchal family, a man has a position subordinate to that of the older woman who heads the household. Often his position is dependent and all too often it is transient. Either way, to exercise authority over his children may bring a man into conflict with the head of the household. One might well speculate that in such families paternal authority means divided authority.

In such a family, a growing boy will have quite a different role model of a man than would another boy who sees his father as the legitimate head of the household. Studies of role models in matriarchal families, in contrast to studies of middle-class white families without a father, are "missing or fragmentary" (Long, 1964). The evidence of psychiatry comes from patients who can afford psychotherapy. These patients come from well-to-do backgrounds and generally from cultures in which the norm is a nuclear family consisting of two parents and their children. The role models must be different in a matriarchal family in which a father is present. How different they are is unknown at the present time.

It is true that there are female heads of households in some white families. In some socioeconomic groups (Miller, 1959) this phenomenon has become institutionalized. For white families, however, this situation is not the group norm in the same way that it is among lower-class Negro families. If the father is present in a lower-class white family, his expected role is that of head of the family, and his wife assumes the role only in his absence. If the father is present in a lower-class Negro family, his presence may mean a divided authority and perhaps an un-wholesome atmosphere for a growing boy (Bell, 1965).

It is also true that a large number of Negro families are both nuclear and middle-class. This fact does not invalidate the argument, but it may explain why the effects of family structure among Negroes did not prove to be independent of family income.

But this explanation is only speculation. There is some in-direct evidence to show that the effect of an absent father is not the same in a Negro family as in a white family. Although this evidence does not prove the theories that are being propounded here, it does allow a degree of confidence in the findings and in the interpretation of them. The first piece of evidence comes from attempts to predict which boys will become delinquent. The concept of delinquency as a form of deviance has led to the concept of concentrating preventive action on predelinquents; Remedial measures were to be applied even before a boy actually committed a violation. Such early measures are only possible if predelinquents can be identified at an early age. Several workers (Glueck and Glueck, 1950; Kvaraceus, 1961) have developed tests based on the characteristics in which delinquents differed from nondelinquents and designed to predict which children would grow up to be delinquents. One such test, that of Sheldon and Eleanor Glueck, was evaluated by the New York City Youth Board, who administered it to a group of children and then observed the children for ten years to assess the accuracy of the prediction (Craig and Glick, 1963; MacDonald, 1965). The test, in five parts, covered four specific relationships between the child and his parents, plus "family cohesiveness." At the end of the ten-year period it became obvious that the test as originally formulated was unsuccessful. "Family cohesiveness" in Negro families had proven to be different from that in white and Puerto Rican families (Gordon, 1963). The criteria for this element of the test needed to be modified for children from Negro matriarchal families. The revised test has not yet had a prospective evaluation, nor can it for many years. At present the available evidence does not reveal the delinquency-producing or delinquency-preventing characteristics in Negro families. But the failure of the Gluecks' original prediction scale is evidence supporting the idea that the effect of family structure on delinquency is different in Negro than in white families.

The second item of evidence comes from a study of high school dropouts (Stetler, 1959). In this study, white dropouts tended to come from one-parent families, but Negro dropouts did not—in fact there appeared to be no great difference between the family structure of Negro dropouts and Negro boys who remained in school. Dropping out of school is not equivalent to delinquency, even though many dropouts are delinquent and many delinquents leave school. Stetler's finding only suggests that the effects of family structure on the actions of a child are not the same in Negro and in white families.

The experimental results described in this chapter and the supporting evidence from other sources can be combined into a new hypothesis: Absence of a parent is an independent factor leading to an increased risk of juvenile delinquency only in a culture in which the norm is a nuclear family. In other cultures it may not be a relevant factor, or it may have an opposite effect. Further studies will be necessary before any definite statements can be made.

If we accept this hypothesis, we not only can say that juvenile delinquency is caused by different factors in different cultures, but we can also say that present methods of delinquency prevention based on family counseling may be inappropriate for Negroes. Not only control methods but even the concepts upon which they are based need reexamination. An earlier section drew the conclusion, based on study of high delinquency rates among Negroes, that the concept of a delinquent as a deviant was faulty. At this point it can be added that the concept that delinquency arises in an unstable home requires at least to be reinterpreted and redefined. An unstable home is not synonymous with a home in which the father is absent. One must ask which characteristics of a home really lead to law-abiding behavior, and the answer is not likely to be simple.

We can no longer assume without proof that the mere existence of a nonnuclear family pattern is "bad." We need to accept families as we find them and learn more about them.

• 5 • THE DECLINE OF THE CORE CITY

Juvenile Hall, in San Francisco, occupies a large, pleasantly landscaped lot at the corner of two wide boulevards about halfway between census tracts R-1 and J-8. On this site are a three-story green concrete office building and nine square cottages that house the delinquent and dependent children receiving detention and shelter care. Besides a maximum-security unit in the main building, four cottages are provided for delinquent boys, two for delinquent girls, and three for neglected children. The children use the small outdoor recreation area and the inadequate classroom in shifts. The facilities have been overcrowded since the mid-1950s. Built in 1950 with a capacity for 195 children, Juvenile Hall had an average daily population of 200 by 1956. The number of inmates rose steadily in subsequent years. Even though the capacity of the institution was increased to 220 in the 1960s, the number of children increased even more rapidly. The statistics (San Francisco Juvenile Court, 1960 and 1964) show more crowding each year from 1956 to 1964. In one month in the latter year the number of juveniles in detention and shelter care rose to 340, more than 150 percent of capacity; at no time during the year did it fall below 100 percent.

As the crowding increased, it became necessary to put two and sometimes even three children into space designed for one. Tempers became short; quarrels became frequent, and staff effort increasingly became custodial rather than rehabilitative.

Overcrowding of detention facilities is only one result of the increase in juvenile delinquency. Not only detention but police, court, and probation services are handling more cases every

year. These conditions constitute a national problem. The
Children's Bureau has pointed out that delinquency has been increasing in urban and suburban areas for half a generation (U.S.
Children's Bureau, 1966), and every year except one since 1949
has seen more adjudicated delinquents and higher delinquency
rates in the United States.

San Francisco statistics have paralleled national statistics. But
San Francisco has had a declining population due to migration
to the suburbs, which have been growing at a tremendous rate.
The paradox of increasing delinquency with a declining population suggests a closer look at what has happened to the population
of the city.

Two years will be compared, 1960 and 1964, in which delinquency statistics were collected by the methods described in
Chapters I and II. Population statistics for 1960 were available
from the national census, but for 1964 had to be estimated.
Standard methods (Bogue and Duncan, 1959) were used to
make this estimate; the methods use birth and death registrations
and school attendance as indicators of population changes and
give an estimate by sex, age, and color. This population estimate
made it possible to calculate migration during the 1960s.

From 1960 to 1964, nearly 13,000 people left the city each
year. (Average net rate. A more precise statement is that during
the four-year period emigration exceeded immigration by
52,000.) About the same number had left each year from 1950
to 1960, so apparently there was no great change in the overall
tendency of central-city dwellers to move to the suburbs. In the
1950s, however, the net figure was the result of an emigration of
14,500 white people per year, which was partially balanced by
an immigration of 3200 nonwhites. In the 1960s, as a result,
fewer white people were left in the city. Even though a slightly
larger percentage were moving out, this was a percentage of the
now smaller white population; in terms of absolute numbers
13,000 a year were leaving. At the same time the flow of nonwhites into San Francisco had slowed to less than a third of the
former rate: 950 per year.

The pattern of the white migration was essentially the same
from 1960 to 1964 as during the 1950s. It consisted of an

emigration of people of all ages except young adults. Each year saw an immigration of about 900 white adults under twenty-five years of age. Presumably these young men and women were attracted to the city by opportunities for employment. But because thousands of white children left the city each year, one can speculate that the young adults, once they married and had children, preferred to bring up their children in the suburbs.

The nonwhite migration pattern did change between 1950 and 1964. In the 1950s nonwhite immigration consisted of people of all ages, from infants to old people. Much of the migration probably occurred early in the decade, when the opportunities for Negroes in Northern cities seemed unlimited and when residential barriers and the pattern of "de facto segregation" had not become apparent. By the end of the decade, the "promised land" did not appear as attractive as it had earlier. In San Francisco the result was a new migration, this time to the suburbs. The effect of urban redevelopment on this new migration pattern has never been measured, but one may assume that destruction of slum housing caused many slum dwellers to leave the city.

The new migration was mainly one of families with children. In the 1950s an average of about 1000 nonwhite children under fifteen entered the city each year, but in the early 1960s about 600 were leaving annually. But the number of nonwhite children in San Francisco did not decrease, for nonwhite birth rates, then as now, were higher than white. In this connection it may be noted that a larger proportion of nonwhite women have been of childbearing age. In other words, nonwhite children were being replaced by newborn nonwhites faster than they were emigrating. In 1965, for the first time, white English-speaking children comprised less than half of the school population. Negroes, Spanish-speaking white children, and Chinese children made up the majority, and school-board projections suggested that the trend would continue, with only a third of the school children in 1970 expected to be both white and English-speaking.

As a result of these and other population changes, the population at risk of becoming delinquent in 1964 was different in many respects from the population at risk in 1960. Because all of the measurable changes were increases in the high-delinquency portions of the juvenile population, the effect on delinquency statistics turned out to be unfavorable.

It has been possible to document four major population changes: (1) an increase in the number of juveniles in the city, (2) a shift in the age distribution of the juvenile population so that a larger proportion of juveniles were at high-delinquency ages, (3) an increased proportion of boys, and (4) an increased proportion of nonwhites. The changes in the population at risk proved sufficient to account for most of the four-year increase in the number of delinquents; the changes are worth examining in detail for they illustrate some of the effects of the changing patterns of living and working that are contributing to the decline of core cities.

The composition of the population at risk in the two study-years is shown in Appendix C. The first changes were in the actual numbers and the ages of juveniles in the city. During the four-year period there was a 7 percent increase in the total juvenile population. Teen-agers accounted for a large part of this increase—so that the 1964 juvenile population contained a substantially higher proportion of adolescents. The population aged fourteen to nineteen had increased 18 percent in four years. Thus, by 1964, there were not only more juveniles, but more of them were at high-delinquency ages.

The next change was in the ratio of boys to girls. In 1960 girls slightly outnumbered boys, but in 1964 the proportion was reversed. The change was small but the high delinquency rates of boys as compared with those of girls explain a large part of the increased number of delinquents.

The last change was an increase in the nonwhite population. This increase was large and in addition was predominantly in the high-delinquency ages.

The importance of these changes is that each change, simply on the basis of risk figures, would be expected to result in an increased number of recorded delinquents. This did indeed occur, in juvenile court cases and in delinquents recorded only by the police department. Altogether, there was a 27.6 percent increase in recorded delinquency in four years.

The shifts in the measurable components of the juvenile

population were not the only changes that were taking place in San Francisco in the early 1960s. The core city is becoming a less attractive place for parents to raise children, but it still contains the most important sources of amusement. The best movies appear first in downtown theaters. Teen-age music halls play the latest popular music. Amusement parks at the beach and the beach itself attract adolescents. The Tenderloin area is the scene of every type of commercial vice, and it is a market-place where teen-agers of both sexes can sell themselves to adults. In addition, gang rivalries and a search for excitement bring automobiles filled with teen age boys into the city looking for trouble. The number of transient boys and girls in the city has probably been increasing, but whether it has or not, the records showed a 14 percent increase in the number of arrests of out-of-town juveniles.

One more population change must be considered. The migra-tion of large numbers of families to the suburbs has an effect on the population remaining behind, and this effect can increase delinquency rates in another way. In general, the migrating families were middle-class. Because middle-class youth are re-corded as delinquent less often than lower-class, the percentage of high-delinquency youths among those left behind necessarily became increasingly greater. This trend cannot be measured without the social and economic data in the decennial census, and no proof will be available until after 1970. Nevertheless, civic leaders are convinced that what has just been described is exactly what is happening, not only in San Francisco but in all our large cities. There are schools in San Francisco where the dis-appearance of the middle class is quite apparent; former middle-class schools now contain lower-class children who bring the school new problems of discipline and poor scholarship.

It is possible to calculate the relative importance of the four measured shifts of population in producing the recorded in-crease of delinquency. This calculation is shown in Table 12. The method of calculation is explained in Appendix B, and I have published a detailed report elsewhere (Eisner, 1967). The cal-culation shows that at least three-quarters of the four-year in-crease could be attributed directly to population changes: 22

percent each to the increase of the juvenile population and the
change in its age distribution, 14 percent to the change in sex
ratio and the remainder to changes in the color distribution of
the juvenile population and to the increase in nonresident cases.
These reasons accounted for two-thirds of the increase in
juvenile court cases.

**Table 12: Percentage of Four-Year Increase in Number of Delinquents
Due To Various Population Changes.**

Reason for Increase	Juvenile Court Cases	All Cases
Increase of juvenile population	22.8%	21.7%
Change in age distribution of juvenile population	18.9	21.8
Change in sex ratio of juvenile population	11.4	14.2
Change in color distribution of juvenile population	15.4	8.9
Change in number of nonresident cases	−1.2	7.9
Remainder, due to other causes	32.7	25.5

The remaining one-quarter of the increase in total delinquency, and one-third of the increase in juvenile-court cases, cannot be explained by measured changes in the population at risk.
Undoubtedly, part of it is due to the shifting social class structure
of the city's population. Even though this trend could not be
measured directly, it is important enough to be investigated
further. This problem was approached by comparing changes in
delinquency in different areas of the city. This step of the investigation could not be done in the way that would have given
the most conclusive answer because of a methodological problem
in defining the population at risk. Generally speaking, the smaller
the population, the less accurate the population estimate. In order
to minimize this error, it was decided to divide the 1964 estimated population into only two parts for the next stage of the
study, even though a division into smaller areas would have
allowed a more detailed answer to questions about changes in
the social class structure of the population.

For this division the city was separated into halves by an
irregular north–south line along census tract boundaries. The
western half of the city was inhabited mainly by a white middle-

class population. It contained three-eighths of the juvenile population. Its forty-one census tracts included all but four of the tracts that were in the highest quartile for income, education, and employment, and none of the tracts that were in the lowest quartile for these indices. The nonwhite population of the western area lived mostly in three census tracts comprising a racially integrated lower-middle-class area.

The eastern half of the city was quite different. It contained all of the census tracts in the lowest quartile for income, education, and employment, and all five of the "poverty areas" that were so designated in 1964 and 1966 by the Office of Economic Opportunity. It also contained the largest of the city's various minority group enclaves—Negro, Spanish-speaking, Chinese, Japanese, and others. Much of the area seemed to be in a state of transition, with middle-class families moving out and lower-class and minority-group families moving in—whereas the entire western area with the possible exception of the racially integrated middle-class area, in which the Negro population was expanding, appeared to be quite stable.

For these two areas, an estimate was made of the number of delinquents there would have been in 1964 if each of the various population groups in each area had become delinquent at 1960 rates. These estimated numbers were then subtracted from the numbers actually recorded in 1964. The results, which are tabulated in Table 13, are expressed as positive numbers if the observed number of delinquents was greater than expected, and negative if it was less. These results apply only to the segment of the total increase that was labeled "Remainder, due to other causes" in Table 12, because the method of estimating the expected numbers made an automatic correction for that part of the increase which was due to population changes.

Several inferences can be drawn from this table. First, it appears that a changing social class structure may well be responsible for some of the increase, because in the stable western area there were either fewer delinquents than expected or only slightly more. Second, delinquency rates among girls appear to be increasing. This increase is a national phenomenon; it is occurring throughout the United States (U.S. Children's Bureau,

Table 13: Differences* Between Observed and Expected Numbers of Delinquents in 1964

| | White | | | | Nonwhite | | | | |
| | MALE | | FEMALE | | MALE | | FEMALE | | |
Interactions	5–13	14–19	5–13	14–19	5–13	14–19	5–13	14–19	Total
Juvenile court only									
Western area	−28	−176	12	11	2	3	−1	10	−167
Eastern area	12	58	27	23	107	181	32	76	516
Total	−16	−118	39	34	109	184	31	86	349
All cases									
Western area	2	−191	19	26	11	−28	7	18	−136
Eastern area	57	−86	45	63	154	222	57	118	630
Total	59	−277	64	89	165	194	64	136	494

* Negative differences indicate observed numbers less than expected numbers.

1966). Third, the largest increase was among nonwhite adolescents.

The last of these three observations is probably the most important. If recorded delinquency rates are increasing in this group, it points to a further deterioration in the relationships between Negro youth and the police, which were discussed in section 1. Either Negro youth were committing more delinquent acts in 1964 than in 1960, or they were perceived by the police as doing so, or both. The evidence from this study is that the situation, which was already bad in 1960, was even worse in 1964.

The trends in delinquency that appeared during the four-year study period show no signs of reversing themselves because the population changes that account for most of the increase are continuing. Each year the number of delinquents becomes larger. Each year more and more of the low-delinquency white middle-class population leaves San Francisco, and each year the population of Negro juveniles increases. As the population of the city changes, the tax base that supports antidelinquency programs becomes smaller. Services become increasingly inadequate. Detention facilities are not the only ones that are overcrowded in San Francisco. The Probation Department budget for 1959–1960 was $1,586,000. Four years later it had been increased to $2,028,000. Nevertheless, the average caseload of probation officers rose during the four years from 112 to 128 boys and from 63 to 73 girls (San Francisco Juvenile Court, 1964). Even though the inadequacy of these important services is recognized, it is visionary to believe that the juvenile court can manage to bring these caseloads down to the recommended maximum of 50 (Krueger, 1960). The significance of a caseload of 128 can be grasped by realizing that it allows a probation officer only an hour and a half each month to try to rehabilitate one delinquent.

If budgets cannot keep pace with the rising number of delinquents, the problem can be handled only by reducing services. Juvenile-court statistics suggest that less time is being given to each case not only by probation officers but also for stays in custody. The average length of stay for a child in custody in San Francisco's Juvenile Hall rose steadily from 1955, when it was 14.7 days, until 1961, when it reached 19.9 days. It then began to fall, however, and in 1964 it was 16.9 days. This drop includes dependent as well as delinquent children; although it may reflect to some extent more efficient handling of cases, it is symptomatic of the inevitable result of the population changes. As the number of delinquents rises, the time and money allotted to delinquency control has to be divided among more individuals, and services to each delinquent are necessarily decreased.

All projections suggest that core cities will continue their present demographic trends. In the future it may confidently be expected that the central areas of our cities will be inhabited by high-delinquency populations and that the low-delinquency middle-class groups will live in suburban rings. The migration patterns of San Francisco suggest that the white middle class is not the only group that likes to live in suburbs. Possibly many suburbs will have an influx of high-delinquency populations. The Negroes who have moved to suburban areas around San Francisco have again found themselves in segregated communities. If they establish relations with the suburban police similar to their present relations with the urban police, delinquency rates will also soar in suburbs. It is more than probable that police and juvenile-court facilities will prove completely inadequate to cope with the rising tide of delinquents. Before this happens, new methods of controlling delinquency must be tried, evaluated, and put into operation.

IV: ENVIRONMENTS CON-
DUCIVE TO
DELINQUENCY

• 1 • THE WORLD OF THE NEGRO GANG BOY

Negro boys whose high delinquency rates have been documented in Chapter III should be the first target of delinquency-prevention programs. Not only is their risk of being labeled as delinquent fantastically high, but also the problem of rising delinquency in American cities is to a great extent the problem of an increasing Negro population in the city centers.

To combat delinquency among Negro boys, the white middle class must take a closer look at the world in which they live, It cannot continue to act from the assumptions that Negro boys live in the same kind of world and that they have the same opportunities as white boys to be successful law-abiding citizens. They do not. If the white middle class attempts to deal with the problem without understanding the special handicaps imposed on Negroes by their environment, it is bound to fail. From childhood on, Negroes are separated from the mainstream of white American culture. They feel isolated, rejected, resentful. Courses of action that appear reasonable to whites do not appear reasonable to them, nor does such action solve the problems of ghetto life. The measures that Negroes adopt to protect themselves from the hostile world in which they find themselves make it more difficult for them to succeed.

Two extremes of behavior used by ghetto Negroes resemble

the behavior of two outstanding types of heroes of American Negro folklore. These types are the trickster and the badman (Abrahams, 1964). White Americans are generally well acquainted with the trickster, for one cycle of folk tales with a trickster hero was adapted into the white culture. This cycle is the collection of stories about Brer Rabbit, as retold a century ago by Joel Chandler Harris. Brer Rabbit is not a clown, nor is he a shiftless ne'er-do-well. He is a true folk hero who overcomes a series of powerful enemies by trickery. Because he cannot overcome his enemies by force, he must win his battles by being clever and by outwitting his foes in each encounter. Brer Rabbit is not eaten by his enemy the wolf; instead, the wolf throws him into a friendly briar patch. R. Abrahams draws a parallel with the situation of the post-emancipation Negro, who could overcome hostile white men only by trickery.

The badman of folklore also overcomes powerful enemies. Unlike the trickster, his method is to use force. Not only is the badman physically powerful, but his presence and behavior are so commanding that they stop his victims from offering any resistance. A quotation from a tale told about "Brother Rabbit" (Abrahams, 1964, p. 77) in Philadelphia in the 1960s will give the spirit and style of these stories.

He feeling sad, downhearted, tears in his eyes. Felt like he was alone in the world. But then he got mad. He said, "I know what I'll do." He went home and shined his shoes, and got his shotgun and went back and kicked the door open. "Don't a motherfucker move." He walked over the table, got all he wanted to eat. Walked over to the bar and got himself all he wanted to drink. He reached over and he grabbed the lion's wife and he dance with her. Grabbed the ape's wife and did it to her. Then he shit in the middle of the floor and he walked out.

The badman and the trickster are found not only in Philadelphia. Stories and toasts about Brother Rabbit, the Signifying Monkey, Stackolee, and other folk heroes in Abrahams' collection are told by "clowns" and "cappers" in New York, Chicago, New Orleans, and Los Angeles, and they have appeared with almost identical wording in San Francisco. They are part of the world of Negro youth all over America. The badman and the trickster illustrate two options of action available to a Negro boy in an urban slum. He can react with guile or with force. Generally he prefers guile, but from time to time, especially in the years when he is establishing his sense of identity, he chooses force.

Psychologically, a teen-ager's most important task is to discover his identity as an adult. From about thirteen to twenty-one, as a boy is developing physically from a child into a man, he must learn who and what he is, and what sort of man he is becoming. The development of this inner knowledge is called the "identity crisis" (Erikson, 1963). This identity crisis must be resolved by boys in every culture, and they usually solve it in groups of their own age. In his group, a boy can experiment with different roles, testing them against the reactions of his friends and of adults. Gradually he discards ineffective roles and "confirms his identity" in whatever role works best for him.

In the slums of our cities, groups of boys form the gangs that are the dominant social institution of Negro adolescents. For the Negro boy in the slums, a search for friends takes him onto the street, which is where he meets other boys. For these boys the street is not a route to be traveled from one place to another; it is itself a "place," where they can meet friends and carry on a large part of their social life. Homes of Negroes in the slums are usually unsuitable for this function. They are generally overcrowded and uncomfortable, and they lack privacy. There are usually no institutions such as gymnasiums and community centers in the ghetto, and those that do exist often make street gang members feel unwelcome. The street is always at hand. C. Brown (1965, p. 415) has stated, "I always thought of Harlem as home but I never thought of Harlem as being in the house. To me, home was in the streets."

The formation of street gangs, however, creates new problems. Many gangs use the street, and conflict between rival gangs is almost inevitable. The typical urban street gang of any race has developed methods of coping with this danger, based on a strong group identity and a readiness to avenge any insult or injury to a member of the gang. Street gang members pride themselves on their loyalty (Brown, 1965, p. 260). In addition, the typical gang has delineated a particular area, the "turf," in which it asserts territorial rights. Within that area a gang member can feel safe from other boys. Outside of it a boy is not safe.

Conflicts between gangs are caused in many different ways. Prominent among them are quarrels over territory and over girls. Regardless of the incident that precipitates a fight, the defensive aspects of these conflicts are impressive. Even a "rumble" to extend a gang's turf is often regarded by the aggressors as a defensive maneuver to protect the gang from encroachments by rival gangs. The gang's turf is understandable if it is interpreted as a defense against real dangers (Jacobs, 1961, pp. 46–50). An invasion of another turf generally is the result of fancied or real provocation.

In this light, even the act of joining the gang can be considered a defensive necessity. When assaulted by superior forces, the boy who does not belong to a gang can do nothing but run. A gang member, on the other hand, can count on his friends to join a fight on his side or to avenge his injuries. In turn he himself is prepared to fight for them.

In his gang a Negro boy must show the approved traits of courage and command of a situation by using force in an approved way (Miller, *et al.*, 1961). The general rule among these fiercely independent and proud boys is that they cannot back down when they are challenged. They may fight, or they may simply show their lack of fear by a studied insolence (Werthman, 1963; Matza, 1964, p. 157). The socially approved role is that of a badman.

This behavior of street gang members tends to bring them into conflict with the police. The use of the street for social intercourse and the emphasis upon fighting are compounded by a gang member's reaction to a challenge by a policeman. The situation is hostile, and, as brought out in Chapter III, it frequently results in actions that deepen the hostility.

A policeman's delinquency-prevention measures necessarily consist of actions that gang boys see as challenges. I. Piliavin and C. Werthman (1967) have described the dilemma. A policeman engaged in crime prevention, as opposed to crime

detection, is searching not for offenders but for potential offenders. They are not impossible to identify. A good policeman knows very well what people are doing in an area he has
under surveillance. He uses several fairly reliable indicators as
guides. One is the type of neighborhood. Another is race. Race
is considered an indicator not because of racial prejudice but
because of past experience: The statistics presented in Chapter
III show that there are good reasons for this approach.

These indicators frequently place a Negro gang boy under
suspicion. Unfortunately, the boy's demeanor when questioned
reinforces a policeman's suspicion. Insolence is possibly more
irritating to a policeman than outright resistance. Thus, the
encounter is almost invariably hostile on both sides. The boy
is confirmed in his opinion that the police are his enemies.
Negro hostility toward policemen does not start, of course, with
random encounters on the street. There are other, far deeper,
reasons whose roots go far back into the history of Negro-white
relations. But the hostility between Negroes and law-enforcement officials is nonetheless a paramount factor in causing high
delinquency rates. The conventional methods of warning and
example do not keep Negro boys from further delinquency; they
often provoke more hostile behavior.

The hostility that permeates police work in a Negro area
carries over into the Negro's relations with every other form of
authority. Werthman (1963) has pointed out, for example,
that the Negro gang boy does not automatically accept the
authority of teachers. The middle-class white student is generally
willing to grant a teacher the right to issue orders, but the
Negro boy considers that the teacher must prove his claim to this
right by demonstrating that he does not misuse it. The boy
expects discrimination and is prepared to react violently when
he meets it. This attitude is responsible for much conflict in
classrooms and is one of the great handicaps that Negro boys,
even very intelligent ones, meet in obtaining an education. Many
boys who want an education actually stay away from school so
that they will not have to face authoritarian teachers.

Most persons who find themselves in a conflict cannot help
but form a theory as to how and why their adversaries function,

and these boys are no exception. They see more than racial discrimination in their conflicts with authority; they see that the actions of those in power contradict what they say. Policemen and teachers claim that the law protects the innocent, but these boys find themselves and their friends interrogated in an unfriendly manner when they are not (at the moment) guilty of any offense. Moreover, they find that they bear the burden of proof to demonstrate their innocence. They feel that policemen (and teachers) should treat them with the respect due to a citizen, but that they are not so treated. As a result, they not only doubt the justice of law enforcement, but regard all white authority (with only an occasional exception) as corrupt. Negro boys suspect white motives to an extent that would be paranoia in middle-class white boys. This is not mental illness: It is a part of Negro culture.

Like adolescent boys in any culture, a Negro street gang member looks to significant adult males in his life to show him how adult men live. Because of his distrust of white authority, it is obvious that his role models will not be successful white men whom he meets, or even middle-class Negroes, whom he calls "Uncle Toms." His role models are adult males of the Negro community, but (as we have already observed) a boy's father is far less likely in Negro than in white families to serve as a role model for his son. A search for a Negro gang boy's role model must start with the question: Where and how do Negro men live in a Negro ghetto?

The 1960 census reports for San Francisco show that there were not as many Negro men as women in the Hunters Point and Fillmore Districts. In Hunters Point approximately 400 fewer men than women were reported. The discrepancy amounted to about one-quarter of all the men between the ages of twenty and forty. These men did not appear on the census report anywhere else in San Francisco; for that matter, they were not reported anywhere. The census figures for the nonwhite population of the entire United States show the same discrepancy. The men are not missing; they are only uncounted. Studies have shown that they reappear in the census as they grow older, because the proportion of sixty- and seventy-year-old men is normal. A publication of the U.S. Department of Labor (1965) discussed the uncounted Negro men and used this finding as part of an argument to show the crisis in the status of Negro family life. For our purposes, we need to ask who these uncounted men are.

The "missing" men are the most visible men in the community. They can be seen on street corners, in front of stores, or in automobiles. They live with friends (male or female) and often have no fixed place of residence. They are visible largely because they do not have jobs that keep them off the street and out of sight.

No one knows the true level of unemployment in Negro ghettoes. Official figures cannot be trusted in a community in which a quarter of the men do not appear in the records, but in San Francisco the statistics showed rates between 10 and 20 percent in 1960. A better estimate would be based on the assumption that the uncounted men all are unemployed and would add them to the official figures. To do so would suggest that at least 40 percent of the men in the ghetto community are not working at any given time. The situation is probably even worse because many Negro men work only at temporary jobs and are soon unemployed again.

Unemployed Negro men are not necessarily destitute. Unemployment is not synonymous with lack of income, even for men whose unemployment insurance has run out. Their income comes from various sources, most of which are illegal. Men who obtain money in these irregular ways are known as "hustlers," and their source of income is a "hustle" (Williamson and Keiser, 1965).

Negro women are better able than Negro men to bring money into the community. Three major ways in which they can do this are through jobs (often as domestic servants), prostitution, and welfare payments. This economic fact determines the form of many hustles. The hustler typically receives his money from these sources, too, but at second hand; for example, by pimping. A common hustle is for a man to persuade a woman to give him money from her welfare check. (The day that welfare checks are distributed is known in many communities as

"Mother's Day".) Other hustles include gambling, pushing drugs, and dealing in stolen goods. There are many more.

Hustlers are the most influential men, in some respects, in the Negro ghetto, and the successful hustler is prominent, well known, and respected. Claude Brown (1965, p. 68) has summed up this attitude in one paragraph:

Bubba said that was how you could tell how slick a nigger was—by how well he did on the street. Butch said Mr. Jimmy, the hustler, was the slickest cat on Eighth Avenue. Mr. Jimmy knew how to "get by" on the street so well that he had never had a job since he left Alabama twenty years before. Mr. Jimmy changed cars every year, dressed up with shining shoes every day of the week, always had plenty of money, always had a pretty woman with him, and kept his hair slicked back.

The successful hustler has some of the qualities of a folk hero. Charles Keil (1966, p. 20) states, "If we are ever to understand what urban Negro culture is all about, we had best view entertainers and hustlers as culture heroes—integral parts of the whole—rather than as deviants or shadow figures." As a folk hero, the hustler resembles the trickster in that he usually operates by guile rather than by force. His stocks in trade are his verbal ability and his ability to find a new hustle when he has a "downfall" in the old one. One should not conclude that the badman cannot also be a hustler; force and sexual prowess are often substituted for cleverness. But it is not a great distortion to equate the successful hustler with the trickster.

The hustler is well known to the gang boy. They frequent the same streets and poolhalls. In the view of the Negro boys in the street gang, the hustler is successful—more so than the man who has a regular job. Most of these boys see hustling as a way of life, and even when they accept employment, they regard their job as another type of hustle.

In the United States today it is difficult for a teen-ager to find a job. Unemployment among teen-agers is usually estimated at twice that of adult unemployment. Generally a boy can obtain employment only through influence of one sort or another. The Negro boy generally has no one to help him get a

job, and if we double our estimate of unemployment among
adult men in the ghetto and say that 80 percent of the out-of-
school Negro gang boys are unemployed, we are probably
erring on the low side. But these boys are exposed to all the
temptations to spend money that an adolescent-conscious ad-
vertising industry can devise. They play the badman role with
authority figures but they become tricksters to satisfy their
economic needs. Generally they obtain money through hustling,
and they are more successful at this than is generally realized. It
is not uncommon for a boy to refuse a position in the Neighborhood Youth Corps at $43.20 per week because he is making
more at his hustle. For example one boy said to me, "Why
should I go for that shit? I can get eighty or ninety dollars on
the street. I won't say how I get it, but I get it."

The hustler is a powerful role model for Negro boys, but
he is not the only one. Middle-class values penetrate the Negro
community and also influence growing boys (Matza, 1964). But
the middle-class pattern of education leading to a career job is
not generally available to a Negro boy in the slums. Schools
are not good; moreover, the boy's attitude toward authority
means that he can go through high school without acquiring
even the equivalent of a middle-class boy's eighth-grade education. Despite the pull of middle-class values, the chances of
failure are so great for the Negro boy who tries to succeed in a
conventional way that most of the gang boys will reject middle-
class aspirations even if suitable role models are available. The
adolescent who chooses a career as a hustler is being a realist,
as was the boy who refused a Neighborhood Youth Corps job.
His estimate of the world he lives in is supported by statistics.
The average income for a nonwhite family with a male head who
had finished high school was $4559 in 1960; the average income
for a similar white family whose head had finished eighth grade
was $4911 (Drake, 1965). The Negro gang boy views school
realistically as a necessary evil rather than as an opportunity
to advance.

To summarize the main features of the world in which most
lower-class Negro boys live: His role models are the tricksters

and the badmen. His career model is the trickster, but his reaction to authority is that of the badman. Despite the pull of
middle-class values, his actions are shaped by the world in
which he finds himself. In this world, a middle-class education
with its false promise of economic security if he graduates from
high school is irrelevant. His world is one in which only the
strong or the clever survive. It is one of injustice, oppression,
and poverty, and it is a world of prostitution, drugs, and theft.

This is why Negro delinquency rates are so high. A boy growing up with badmen and tricksters as his role models, and who
solves his identity crisis in a street gang that is constantly at war
with the community's authority structure, becomes a delinquent in order to fit into his own culture (Hill, 1959). It is
futile to advise him that he can become a "success" in middle-
class terms. First, the chances are overwhelming that he cannot
succeed, because to do so he usually must overcome not only
racial discrimination but also an inadequate education and a
police record. Second, this type of success would separate him
from his friends and cut him off from the environment in which
he grew up.

This situation, when translated into a delinquency-prevention
program, calls for a radical approach to the lower-class Negro
delinquent. Possible approaches will be discussed in another
chapter. But the essentials of an antidelinquency program are
clear: It must diminish the hostility between the Negro boy and
the police. It must persuade him to aspire to a career of work
rather than a hustle—but in addition it must provide him with
a real opportunity for employment. The program must do more
than change the boy; it must change the social and economic
structure of the Negro community.

• 2 • THE ALL-WHITE SUBURB

Not all delinquents are Negro gang boys, although their situation is so appallingly bad that it must be our first priority. Middle-class white youth also become delinquents, and although
white delinquency rates are only a fraction of the Negro rates,
there are so many more white juveniles that the delinquents

among them far outnumber Negro delinquents. In 1960, 57 percent of the delinquent population of San Francisco were white, and only half as many were Negro. A third of these white delinquents were from all-white middle-class areas.

Delinquent activity by middle-class youths is grossly under-reported in police and court records. There are many ways in which the community can handle undesirable behavior besides police and court action.] As mentioned in Chapter III, if a family is intact, it is often sufficient to report a boy's behavior to his father, who will make restitution or institute appropriate dis-ciplinary action. Often professional resources such as the schools, physicians, psychiatrists, or ministers can help with mis-behaving children. Even so, an appreciable proportion of mid-dle-class children are handled by law-enforcement officials and are labeled as delinquents. Moreover, adolescents in middle-class communities are forming their own "youth culture," with customs and values that differ so markedly from those of their parents that one commonly hears young people say, "Don't trust anyone over thirty." The differences that are obvious to adults, such as hair and clothing styles or tastes in music, are not the only ones. Adolescents today are using dangerous and illegal drugs such as marijuana and LSD. Often they defy the law with mass demonstrations against a government or a school policy. Their sexual habits have led to an alarming incidence of venereal disease and pregnancy. Middle-class delinquency has become an important phenomenon of our time.

Delinquency was only one of the subjects considered by a conference of adolescents held in 1965 under the sponsorship of the governor of California. At this conference several thou-sand youths of high-school age, from all areas of northern California, met to discuss their problems. The delegates were largely middle-class; a small contingent of Negro boys from Hunters Point in San Francisco found themselves in demand at all of the discussion sessions, simply because most of the delegates had never had the opportunity to meet members of this group. The delegates made a total of 64 recommendations, ten of which especially pertain to middle-class delinquency:

EDUCATION

Students . . . be given more responsibility for student affairs

Students be involved in setting school standards and rules
through youth councils

PARTICIPATION IN COMMUNITY ACTION

Schools and youth organizations be encouraged to involve students more actively in problems concerning the community

A program be devised to give youth a voice in community government (perhaps an elected youth official)

Youth be involved in civic projects for which they would receive recognition

Youth serve on committees with adults

Youth serve in youth-serving organizations to bridge the gap
between the adults in the agency and the recipients of the
services of the agency

JOBS

School curriculum . . . be expanded to expose all students to
the world of work, particularly college-bound students

Job opportunities be developed for all youth, not just dropouts

Students be included as members of school or district committees working with the industrial community to develop youth
employment opportunities.

These ten recommendations expressed what these adolescents
were trying to say to the adults at the conference. Student leaders
from middle-class homes were especially eloquent in expressing
these thoughts in discussion groups. The ten recommendations
add up to a plea by the youth of California to be allowed to
take part in our society and to participate in matters that concern them. Their plea constitutes a condemnation of just those
aspects of the American way of life that are causing a large part
of the delinquency problem in the middle class.

This chapter will discuss the problem to which the young
people at the conference were addressing themselves. This problem is the barrier, inherent in the structure of our society, that
keeps youth out of all meaningful adult activity. The barrier is
a result of the adult assumption that only adults know what is

best for youth, and its effect is to increase juvenile delinquency among middle-class adolescents.

The barrier is formed by three characteristics of the middle-class child's environment—characteristics that together constitute a strong social force encouraging the development of a distinct adolescent subculture. These characteristics are segregation by age, institutionalized social life, and a lack of alternate pathways to success.

Segregation by age has resulted from a general recognition that children need the company of other children. In the school years from six to twelve, a child's psychological task (Erikson, 1963) is to develop a "sense of industry." This is analogous to the "sense of identity" that an adolescent develops and which was discussed in section 1. If he fails to develop a sense of industry, E. H. Erikson names the alternative "inferiority": the sense of personal inadequacy that develops if a child does not receive recognition for his efforts. The school-age child develops his sense of industry by his successes in doing and making things. Usually he obtains these successes in competition with others of his own age. Basically, the reason for dividing school children into grades, or for dividing baseball teams into age groups, is to provide each child with appropriate competition so as to give him a chance for his due share of successes. For the same reason an age-graded school may be divided into ability-graded sections.

But a school-age child needs more than competition with his peers. Like the adolescent, he needs role models. The six-year-old needs to see how seven-year-olds act so that he in turn will be a successful seven-year-old. The seven-year-old needs to observe eight-year-olds, and so on. The child also needs an opportunity to react with adults. In infancy, a child needs one adult, his mother. Later he needs many adults—both of his parents, his teachers, and all of the people who make up his community. With these psychological necessities in mind, let us look at the middle-class suburb to see what opportunities a child has.

The most prominent feature of suburban life is the isolation of individual families. The ideal of the American middle class is for each nuclear family to own its own home, preferably one that has large open areas, both indoors and outdoors, in which children can play. Each home is occupied by a mother and her preschool children during the day and by two parents and all the children at night. Grandparents and other relatives live elsewhere. The composition and ages of neighboring families are usually similar, so that a child finds children of the same age to play with when he is not engaged in a scheduled activity. The suburban home is reached by automobile, and nearly all excursions away from home require the car. Very few suburban children can be sent to the store for a loaf of bread.

A child living in such a home finds that his life away from it is carefully scheduled and supervised. His mornings and part of each afternoon are spent in school. After school he may have one of many types of additional education, such as music lessons, or he may join a group activity, such as a supervised athletic session or a supervised recreation session. Occasionally he may engage in free play with his contemporaries. On weekends, he usually accompanies his parents in a family activity.

An important feature of this life is the extent to which activities are arranged so that the children who participate in them are all of the same age. Practically no organized activity except baby-sitting puts adolescents in contact with school-age or preschool children. A child's contacts with adults are generally restricted to his parents, substitute parents, and teachers. As a child grows older, this age segregation continues. Adolescents find teen-age centers, teen-age clinics, teen-age dances, and teen-age conferences to discuss the problems of teen-agers. They rarely find an activity in which they can participate in the company of adults. One might imagine that our society hates children, for we have carefully arranged that only parents and people employed for the purpose have any contact with them. In many cultures old people play an important role as the natural teachers of children. In the typical suburb they are not present, because segregation by age is not limited to children. We also have a variety of methods for segregating and isolating old people.

The necessary and meaningful work of our society is carried

on by the population of young and middle-aged adults. Children and adolescents do not participate in this work; they are restricted to activities designed to prepare them for adult life. They carry on these activities in groups with an age spread of only a few years.

The physical conditions of middle-class housing also affect the child's social life. Suburban life requires an institutionalized rather than a spontaneous pattern of socialization. Children meet each other and engage in social activities by prearrangement and on a rigid time schedule. If David wants to visit Scott, he or his mother must first phone to see whether Scott will be home. Then David's mother drives him to Scott's house, saying, "I'll pick you up at quarter-to-five. Be ready to go when I ring the doorbell because we have to pick up Marcia at her dancing class at five sharp and then I have to get home and start supper." Scott lives too far away for David to walk over, and the dancing class is several miles from Marcia's home. Mother spends a large portion of her day on such errands, because they must all be done in the automobile, which only she can drive. She must keep to a rigid schedule if she is to accomplish her tasks at all.

But few of a suburban child's activities are even as spontaneous as David's visit to Scott. Many activities for children in middle-class communities take place at certain times of certain days. Some of these activities, such as Cub Scouts and Little League, are supervised by parents. Some, such as park-department recreation and athletic periods, are supervised by adults hired for the purpose. Like attendance at school, the activities are entered into by prearrangement and according to a schedule. The thoughts of youth are no longer "long, long thoughts"— modern children have little time left for daydreaming. Until a child is old enough to command his own wheeled transportation, he is confined to the schedule imposed by Mother's automobile. The independence that allows children spontaneous, unplanned meetings may come with possession of bicycles at seven or eight years of age. In many areas a bicycle is unsafe because of heavy automobile traffic, and independence arrives only with a driver's license.

The institutionalization of social life is beneficial in that children are kept safely away from many hazards. They do not play on the streets, they are not long out of the sight of adults. This institutionalization has a corresponding disadvantage in that children are relentlessly guided into conformity to the customs of our society. They have no choice concerning the part of society they are expected to enter. They are being prepared to earn high incomes and to establish middle-class homes in which they will repeat the lives of their parents.

The institution that primarily enforces middle-class conformity is the school, and other institutions perform a supporting role. It may well be said that next to his parents school is the most powerful influence to which the middle-class child is exposed.

In recent years it has become fashionable to criticize schools. On the one hand, their failures to deal adequately with lower-class children are deplored, and, on the other, it is pointed out that middle-class children are deficient in mathematics, reading, or some other subject which has attracted popular attention. These criticisms neglect the undoubted fact that our schools are designed in accordance with middle-class standards to educate middle-class children, and that when they are able to confine themselves to this task, they do a remarkably good job. They are to be criticized, I believe, for what is a consequence of this very success: They have become so much a part of the socialization of middle-class children that there is no longer any alternate route.

For a middle-class boy, success in school is absolutely essential. If he is not well prepared in grammar school, he will be unable to succeed in high school. If he does not finish high school, he will be unemployable. His stakes in high school are even greater than a lower-class boy's, for he needs not only a diploma, but also high grades in order to get into college. Success in the middle-class world depends more and more upon a college education.

There is no other choice for the middle-class child who wishes to enter the world in which his parents live. Admission to it requires him to have the education now considered necessary for middle-class employment, and he can get this education only from high schools and colleges. He can no longer leave high school and go into a lower-class occupation, for this too requires at least a high-school education. There is no longer a system by which a boy who is unable or unwilling to do well in school can enter an apprenticeship or a job at a beginner's level from which he can rise according to his ability. To repeat, success in school is the only available route.

Middle-class parents are well aware of this. They have fashioned a world that gives their children the best possible chance to succeed in school. They have moved, at the cost of considerable commuting inconvenience, to the all-white suburbs whose schools contain only middle class children. They have organized car pools, cooperative nursery schools, children's athletic leagues, youth centers, and all the time-consuming activities that keep their children in the company of other children of similar background. Parents' efforts to organize children into age groups, to institutionalize their lives, and to motivate them into succes in the educational system are designed to ensure that they will grow into adults well prepared to enter middle-class occupations. In short, middle-class adults have very efficiently and with the best of motives excluded children and adolescents from all adult activities.

E. Z. Friedenberg (1963) has compared the social system we have for our youth to a colonial system. He states (p. 181), "Teenagers, prisoners, and mental hospital patients are helpless in the toils of their respective institutions. By definition they are there for their own good." His analogies are apt. An adolescent is confined in a network of laws, regulations, and customs based on the middle-class patterns of preparation for life in a middle-class world. The purpose of this network is to ensure that he completes an adequate preparation for adult life, but its effect, in many cases, is to encourage juvenile delinquency. To understand why, we must take our eyes off the long-range goals of parents and look at what this system does for the immediate needs of adolescents.

From this point of view, the entire social system might have been designed to keep adolescents out of the productive segment of society. As already pointed out, the adolescent has no opportunity to have a significant relationship with any adult besides his parents and teachers. He cannot work, except at odd jobs that have no relation to his subsequent career, and, living in the suburbs, he cannot even watch his commuter father work. Suburban children have very little concept of how their fathers actually earn money, but they learn early in life that this work is important and fascinating, like the apples on a tree that hang out of reach. A child who is developing a sense of industry can only do so by succeeding at children's tasks. He is not allowed to try his hand at any economically meaningful work.

Children learn that adults have other privileges besides that of employment: Adults are mobile, for they can drive; they are allowed the privilege of sex; they are permitted drugs, such as tobacco and alcohol, which alter mood and state of consciousness; and they are able to go where they please at any hour. These, like work, are all privileges denied to adolescents while they are striving to become adults.

An adolescent has four options regarding these privileges. He can, of course, wait and enjoy them later. Deferred gratification is an important middle-class value. He is expected to wait, and on the whole most adolescents do. For most this choice leads to a rewarding life. But an adolescent who cannot or will not wait has three other choices, all undesirable. He may assume adult status and privileges before he has completed his education, or he may rebel against the middle-class social system. As a final choice he has suicide, which is appallingly frequent among adolescents (Bruyn and Seiden, 1965; McNassor, 1967).

Our culture contains no *rites de passage*. There is no functional ceremony that marks the point at which a boy becomes a man. Confirmation and Bar Mitzvah are anachronisms that entitle a boy to an adult status only in ceremonial functions. The only statuses a boy (or girl) can voluntarily assume that carry adult privileges are marriage and parenthood. Thus, many adolescents in middle-class communities marry before they complete their education and so acquire adult rights to sexual intercourse and a certain control over their own activities.

Instead of marriage, a nonconforming adolescent may choose rebellion. Typically rebellion is aimed at what appear to be the dominant values in the suburb: money and education. The adult "rat race" for high income and status is condemned, and (at least at the present time) nonmaterial, spiritual values are substituted. These may be Zen Buddhism, a crusade for civil rights, or an attempt for "meaningful relationships." On the other hand, the rebellion may be directed at the school itself. Regardless of the current fashion, the rebellion includes a denial of the validity of the usual suburban ideals.

Rebellion is highly functional for many young people, especially when it can be carried on with the support of a like-minded group. Group rebellion allows conformity to the standards of an alternate social system, which often can be described as a youth culture. An adolescent who conforms to the values of the current youth culture solves a number of problems at one stroke. His problems of success in school and obtaining a good job are solved by rejecting the necessity for either. The problem of sex is solved by rejecting society's sanctions in favor of sex as an expression of a meaningful relationship. A desire to experiment with drugs becomes a new "drug culture" (Blumer, *et al.*, 1967), in which the alterations of consciousness produced by LSD, methedrine, or marijuana are seen as important self-fulfilling experiences.

It is not being argued here that teen-agers should marry or that the use of LSD should be encouraged. Early marriage (and illegitimate pregnancies and venereal disease) and the growing use of dangerous drugs seem to be the consequences of a refusal to allow adolescents to participate in adult activities and of restricting them to only one legitimate pathway to success. Even though this pathway is a good one, it is obvious from the reaction of adolescents that it cannot be perfect, nor can it fit the needs of all middle-class youth. Adults must, in view of the results, admit that they do not, in many cases, really know what's best for their children.

The recommendations of the Governor's Conference on Youth are a cry for help. Adolescents are asking to be allowed to participate in American society, not (to use Friedenberg's analogy) as colonial subjects, but as participants. They want an opportunity to influence their own lives. If this opportunity is denied them, it leaves the independent spirits, the malcontents, and the incapable among them no legitimate pathway to success, and it encourages them to find their own ways outside of the system society has imposed. In our present system all options other than waiting for future gratification are defined as illegal or immoral. For this reason I consider the barrier to participation in adult life as the major cause of middle-class delinquency.

In many ways the situation of the middle-class white adolescent resembles the situation of the lower-class Negro in our society. Like the Negro, the adolescent belongs to a minority group that is prevented from sharing in all the benefits of our society. The benefits sought by each group are different, but the fact of exclusion is the same. Like the lower-class Negro adolescent, the middle-class white adolescent is isolated from the adult role models our culture considers most appropriate. The Negro, who is allowed more freedom, finds his role models in the poolhalls and on the streets. The suburban white boy may find his role models in literature, on television, in his school, or elsewhere, but (again like the Negro) his role model cannot be the man at work because the boy is not allowed to enter the world of work. Like the Negro, the white boy tries out various roles among his contemporaries; his insulation from adults makes him especially prone to develop his own culture, however, rather than to conform to the culture around him.

The solution to the problem of a separate culture of youth is to absorb it into the general culture of adults. Such a process is what the youth at the governor's conference wanted, and I submit that most middle-class adults would also prefer it. To achieve it, we must do as young people themselves suggest: We must devise mechanisms whereby youth can make its opinions known to adults. But we must go even farther if we want to change youth cultures. We must give adolescents the opportunity to make their own decisions in matters that affect them. We must even give them the option of making decisions we do not like. To protect our children from disastrous choices, we should provide a variety of pathways all of which can lead to a worthwhile place in society. Adolescents badly need mechanisms for entering adult life (similar to an apprenticeship system) that can serve as alternatives to conventional education.

Middle-class delinquency would not disappear if we allowed teen-agers to participate in adult activities and if we provided an alternative pathway to a working life. But these steps would remove much of the pressure that is driving our children into nonconformity. If young people could choose any of several conventional pathways, far fewer of them would be forced into delinquency.

V: THE DEVIANT
DELINQUENT

Americans cannot quite decide whether delinquents are sick or bad. We are not sure whether they should be treated by psychiatrists or severely punished. This indecision is apparent in the mechanisms we use to handle delinquents. The juvenile-court concept of rehabilitation—through medical and social experts or through effective use of probation—conflicts with the older philosophy that punishment is necessary to deter delinquents and their associates from further wrongdoing.

In this book I am presenting the concept that most delinquents are neither sick nor bad; they are simply members of abnormal groups in our society. There are delinquents who are abnormal members of their own groups, however. These delinquents are deviants who are in need of medical or psychiatric treatment. Their problems will not be solved by punishment or by measures designed to change the society they live in.

A boy I met many years ago is an example of a deviant delinquent. Tom was fifteen years old the year he attended my pediatric convulsive clinic. He was tall for his age, nearly adult size, with a shock of blond hair and an engaging smile. He attended a local high school and made poor grades. He was well known to the police and to the juvenile court. When he first came to me, he was on probation for frequent fighting. During the year I knew him he was transferred to another school, for disciplinary reasons. His performance in the new school was no better than in the old. About a year after I met him he was sent to an institution for delinquents, and I never saw him again.

Tom's delinquency was caused by a neurological problem. He was suffering from a condition called psychomotor epilepsy, which in his case could be only partially controlled by anticonvulsant drugs. When he took no medication, he had seizures that began with about two seconds of mumbling and vague arm waving, followed by convulsive movements and unconsciousness lasting five or ten minutes. After a convulsion he would be sleepy for about an hour. When he was placed on the largest dose of medication he could tolerate, he no longer had these seizures, but he had other manifestations of epilepsy, which proved in the long run to be equally handicapping. At intervals of a week or so he would have a distinct alteration of mood and become argumentative and belligerent. These episodes were liable to occur in almost any surroundings, and generally they led to the fighting that had brought him to juvenile court. Tom rarely remembered these fights, and usually learned what had happened only when someone told him later. His amnesia for these events was evidence that the episodes were manifestations of his epilepsy, and this evidence was supported by his electro-encephalogram.

Tom was not the only psychomotor epileptic in my clinic who was a delinquent. His case stands out because it was clear-cut, but there are many adolescents with this form of convulsive disorder who act in ways that may cause trouble with the police (Bingley, 1958, *passim*). These adolescents are truly deviant delinquents. Their behavior is not caused by the pressures of society or by the demands of their culture. It is at variance with the normal standards of the group to which they belong. In Tom's case, his actions resulted from physical illness. In other cases, deviant behavior may occur because an individual is mentally retarded or because he is suffering from mental illness.

Physical and mental illness may occur in all degrees of severity. The extreme and obvious forms are not difficult to recognize, but the mild forms can present problems of diagnosis and may even remain undiscovered. My patient, Tom, had a form of brain damage that may well have been due to an injury incurred at the time of birth. (Many would dispute this statement; however, see Lilienfeld and Pasamanick, 1954; Earle, Baldwin, and Penfield, 1953.) Birth injuries vary enormously in severity: They may cause death or, in descending order of severity, cerebral palsy, epilepsy, or so-called minimal brain damage. In addition, they may impair specific functions such as speech or reading. The severely brain-injured child may be grossly retarded, whereas the child with only a slight brain injury may have no disability except a short attention span.

Let us consider the case of a boy who has normal intelligence but who has a specific reading disability due to birth injury. He will appear completely normal in infancy and early childhood. At about seven years of age he will begin to have difficulties in school. At first this will be apparent only because his spelling is poor—he may even be able to get good marks by memorizing passages and associating them with the illustrations in his primer. But as time goes on, he will fall farther and farther behind his classmates. Even when it becomes apparent that he is a "poor student," his specific reading disability is likely to go undiagnosed for many years. Typically such a boy is given the special tests necessary to diagnose his disability only after several years of difficulty, and all too often this step is never taken. Eventually he may leave school.

Brain damage is not always the reason for a reading disability (Glaser and Clemmens, 1965). When a reading disability is discovered, the cause must be diagnosed before any treatment is possible. No one knows how many children have specific reading disabilities due to brain damage, because too few children receive intensive investigation. A reading disability may be due to an emotional disorder or to cultural deprivation. Whatever its cause, a reading disability itself may produce emotional problems. The diagnosis of reading problems calls for a skilled physician, a psychologist, and several other specialists. Diagnostic teams capable of tracking down all possible causes of a reading difficulty are few and far between (Gordon, 1966).

Thus, it is unlikely that a boy with a specific reading disability will be correctly diagnosed. Quite probably his reading disability will lead to failure in school. This failure may lead him, by one of the routes described in Chapter IV, into delinquency. In the same way, any child with brain damage may eventually be labeled as a delinquent.

The evidence relating brain damage to delinquent behavior is unsatisfactory and even contradictory. Two studies on epilepsy among delinquents can be cited. N. L. Low and S. P. Dawson (1961) studied the electroencephalograms of one hundred successive adjudicated second offenders. Twenty-nine of the electroencephalograms showed a certain abnormality (fourteen and six per second positive spikes), but Low and Dawson did not study a control group, and no one is quite sure how often this abnormality would occur in nondelinquents. In a similar study, S. D. Loomis (1965) did electroencephalograms on 150 delinquent boys and found only 100 normal. An abnormal electroencephalogram does not prove the presence of epilepsy. Despite the large number of abnormalities they found, neither study was able to demonstrate psychomotor epilepsy nor, for that matter, any other form of this disease as a cause of delinquency. One may infer that even if many psychomotor epileptics are delinquents, few delinquents suffer from this rare condition.

The evidence on milder forms of brain damage is even more unsatisfactory. For example, E. Oppenheimer and M. Mendel (1959) studied children with behavior disturbances who had been referred to school diagnostic facilities; they found that 20 percent of the referrals were children whom they believed to have brain damage. On the other hand, Lucas, *et al.,* (1965) found a "negative correlation" between antisocial behavior and neurological damage.

It is more difficult to diagnose neurosis and relate it to delinquency than it is to diagnose brain damage. Even if a mental illness is present, we have no clear-cut method of diagnosis that can tell us that it is the cause of the delinquent behavior. Emotional problems are often diagnosed on the basis of the actions of the patient. This method can lead to a type of circular reasoning, in which the delinquent act itself is considered the proof of mental illness and the only task then is to identify the particular type of neurosis. Any mild deviation of the delinquent's family from the customary emotional pattern may often be interpreted as the "cause" of delinquency. But if the delinquent act itself is not considered in the diagnosis, whatever evidence of mental illness remains may indicate nothing worse than the problems of many nondelinquent children.

Nevertheless, emotional problems are at the root of much delinquent behavior. Adelaide Johnson (1956) has described the role of parents, who may unconsciously encourage behavior they verbally forbid, and T. E. Schaffer (1961) has tried to distinguish between sociological and psychiatric causes of delinquency. The U.S. Children's Bureau (1955), in a booklet on the use of health services to prevent delinquency, presents the argument that delinquency is a manifestation of poor mental health in children who are unable to control their aggressive feelings. My own results can be interpreted to support the importance of the emotional atmosphere of the home in the genesis of delinquency: section 4 of Chapter III showed that the absence of a parent more than doubled the risk of delinquency for white children in high-income census tracts.

The concept that delinquency is usually due to emotional problems is not as popular as it used to be. W. Healy and A. F. Bronner could point in 1936 to unsatisfactory interpersonal relations within families as the major cause of delinquency, and they could consider the extrafamilial environment to be of only "contributory" importance. Since that time many sociological studies have shown the effect of gangs, slums, and other influences outside of the home. Nevertheless, there is no reason to throw out the psychiatric evidence indicating that many youths engage in antisocial behavior because of attitudes acquired in their homes. Yet family situations that could lead to delinquency can instead lead to other types of difficulty that are not labeled as delinquent, whereas a mild and self-limited problem in an adolescent boy's search for identity may lead him to a dramatic and highly illegal act such as a robbery. The severity of a neurosis does not determine the illegality of actions that result from it.

Two studies give fairly authoritative estimates of how much delinquency is due to individual pathology. Kvaraceus *et al.* (1959, p. 54) estimated that only 25 percent of delinquents were emotionally disturbed and that the behavior of the remainder should be attributed to cultural factors. The California Youth Authority (1967) classified an experimental group of 627 first offenders (excluding "seriously assaultive cases and cases to which there is a community objection") into categories based on their "interpersonal maturity level" and their way of responding to their perceptions of their world. There were nine categories, three of which accounted for over half of the cases: one of these three was labeled "Asocial, Aggressive"; one, "Neurotic, acting out"; and one, "Neurotic, anxious." Because diagnosis of these conditions is so subjective, it is not clear how much trust can be placed in these estimates. Nevertheless, some degree of mental illness is certainly found in a substantial number of delinquents.

There are other types of delinquents whose delinquency is quite obviously due to physical or mental illness. A heroin addict who steals to support his "habit" is an example. Although he may have begun to use heroin because of sociological pressures, once he has become addicted it is the necessity to obtain an illegal and expensive drug that forces him to steal. Another example is a homosexual prostitute, of whom there are an estimated 200 in San Francisco (Hansen, Forrester, and Bird, 1966). Drug addiction and homosexual prostitution are especially difficult social problems, which medical or psychiatric treatment is probably unable to alter. But treatment can be effective in other cases. For example, children with epilepsy can be treated with anticonvulsant drugs, children with reading problems can be given special education, and children with neuroses can receive psychotherapy.

American culture in general allows much latitude to people whose behavior is due to illness, whether physical or mental. A person who is ill is expected to cease his normal activities and to take steps that will restore him to health. Not only is he expected to do so, but our society contains a variety of mechanisms that help him do so—for example, sick leave and medical clinics. People are not to be punished for illness, they are to be cured. Before they can be cured, however, they must be identified as being ill. This requirement leads to the question of whether delinquency prevention and management should depend to any great extent on the diagnosis and treatment of the deviants in the delinquent population.

As a first step, we can consider whether these deviants are really more common among delinquents than they are in the general population of juveniles. We have the evidence of one extensive study that compared delinquents and nondelinquents. Glueck and Glueck (1950) examined 500 delinquents and 500 nondelinquents. These delinquents were all institutionalized multiple offenders, a group of boys who not only had been labeled as delinquents, but also had committed acts that any reasonable person would consider antisocial. The nondelinquents were boys attending public school; they were matched to the delinquent boys by age, IQ, ethnic background, and area of residence. Not only had the nondelinquents never been labeled as delinquents, but only a quarter of them had ever committed an act for which they might have been classified as delinquent. Neither group included Negroes.

The Gluecks discovered that the delinquents were healthier both mentally and physically than the nondelinquents! Evidence of mental illness was determined by psychiatrists who did not know if the subjects were delinquents or nondelinquents. When the groups were examined for evidence of psychoneurosis, 25 percent of the delinquents and 36 percent of the nondelinquents were judged to be neurotic. Only 0.4 percent of the delinquents, compared with 1.6 percent of the nondelinquents, showed any signs of psychotic traits. The one area in which more mental illness was found among delinquents was "psychopathy," which was diagnosed in 7.3 percent of the delinquents and only 0.4 percent of the nondelinquents. It is true that there was more evidence of emotional conflict in the delinquents. This evidence was found in three-quarters of the delinquents and in slightly over one-third of the nondelinquents; moreover, the delinquents as a group were more likely to have disturbed relationships within their families.

In the area of physical health, the delinquents were generally stronger, better developed, and less liable to fall ill than the non-delinquents. A thorough and painstaking neurological examination showed some degree of abnormality in 73 percent of the nondelinquents but in only 64 percent of the delinquents.

On the basis of this evidence it is hard to justify a delinquency program based on medical and psychiatric treatment. Although many delinquents, like the boy whose story I told at the beginning of the chapter, are deviants who need this kind of treatment, the Gluecks' study tells us that we would do better to find such children without reference to their delinquency. We should not look for psychomotor epileptics among delinquents, but among all children; for example, in schools. If a delinquent has a neurosis, he should be treated, but it should not be necessary for him to become a delinquent to be eligible for treatment. A child with a reading disability should be brought to the attention of a diagnostic team because he cannot read, not because he has violated a law.

We have not been successful in modifying the behavior of delinquents by psychiatric means (Craig and Furst, 1965; Adamson and Dunham, 1956). Actually, any treatment of delinquents as such may increase delinquency. The reason is that the mere fact of the treatment "confirms" the boy or girl in the role of a delinquent. Adolescents try many roles in their search for identity. Erikson and Erikson (1957) were apparently the first to point out that adolescents eventually form the concept of their own identity from the reactions of adults to the roles they try. When adults decide that a boy or girl "is" a delinquent, the labeling process itself may persuade the adolescent that his true identity is that of a delinquent. He then acts in the way he is expected to act in that role—that is, as a delinquent. Lentz (1966) has pointed out the paradox thus created for delinquency treatment agencies: They must label a boy as a delinquent and thereby risk confirming him in a delinquent role before they can institute the treatment designed to move him to another role.

The successes of psychiatry and medicine in delinquency control have actually been in the area of preventing delinquency labeling (Stapleton, 1962). They have been able to provide a youth with an alternate interpretation of his identity. A boy whose misbehavior is handled by sending him to juvenile court is confirmed in his identity as a delinquent, but if the same boy had been brought to a psychiatrist he could have adopted the role of a patient and addressed himself to the activity appropriate to such a role—to get well.

Labeling an offender as a patient rather than as a delinquent is often the means of handling antisocial behavior in middle-class communities. It is probably this method and other alternates to delinquency labeling that cause the marked discrepancy between lower-class and middle-class recorded delinquency that was discussed in section 3 of Chapter III. In retrospect, Tom's delinquency can be considered a failure of medical treatment in the sense that I, his physician, did not communicate my interpretation of his case to his school and to his community. Tom should certainly have been given a different label than that of a delinquent. His behavior was judged to be intolerable in his community, but the solution the community adopted, that of institutionalization, was not one that helped him to become a productive adult. The lesson for delinquency prevention is that the deviant delinquent can often be handled in ways other than labeling him as a delinquent. We need to change society's way of handling children more than we need to change the children.

Medical and psychiatric facilities are less available to lower-class than to middle-class children, and they are less utilized. A program of treating deviant delinquents should be aimed at children who exhibit aberrant behavior in school, and it should be begun before they are labeled delinquents. For its maximum effect the program should be concentrated in lower-class areas. Its purpose should be to prevent delinquency labeling of sick children.

VI: THE CONTROL OF DELINQUENCY

• 1 • REDUCTION OF GROUP ALIENATION

Although both punishment and rehabilitation have a place in delinquency control, neither is effective as it is currently used. Punishment has reached a point of diminishing returns where its effect is to increase the alienation of large segments of the juvenile population, and rehabilitation based on the concept that a delinquent is mentally ill is ineffective for the large proportion of delinquents who can be described as normal members of a deviant society.

In this chapter delinquency control will be discussed on the premise that the majority of delinquents are neither sick nor mentally disturbed, but that they are alienated from our dominant culture. This premise implies that delinquency control requires massive and expensive programs extending into many areas of community life and requiring coordination of the work of many agencies. The programs must be designed to change the structure of the world in which adolescents live, as well as to change the adolescents themselves.

Many of the conventional methods now in use require broad community-based activities, but all are founded on the theory that the delinquent is a deviant. This theory demands that delinquents themselves be the targets of control programs and that predelinquents be the targets of prevention. In my opinion these programs have not worked and indeed cannot. Not only have rising delinquency rates in the United States and elsewhere shown clearly that the "deviant delinquent" theory has led to failure, but formal program evaluation has shown this also (Witmer and Tufts, 1954). The failure has been so evident that it has led one observer (Tunley, 1962, pp. 31ff.), who observed the field as a journalist rather than as a social scientist, to doubt whether science was capable of solving the problem.

Many authors have described conventional delinquency-control methods. R. M. MacIver (1966) has written one of the most thorough descriptions, in which he calls for better overall planning, more effective and better trained personnel, and integration of the programs of many agencies. He recommends neighborhood-focused programs, work experience for students, and a friendly attitude of the police toward the public. His concept of the services for adjudicated delinquents is nonpunitive, and the measures he recommends are based on rehabilitation rather than on punishment. His views are shared by all but a few of the experts in his field. Nevertheless, his book contains no suggestion that society may be producing delinquency, nor does he ever suggest that the delinquent may be acting normally in the world in which he lives. Thus all the methods he recommends are designed to change adolescents rather than their environment.

Many of my recommendations resemble those of MacIver. Nevertheless, the studies reported in this book show that delinquency is far too common among members of high-risk groups to say that delinquents are deviants. Delinquency is not due to poverty per se, for it is highest in low-middle income groups. It is not due primarily to abnormal family structure, for among high-delinquency Negro youths delinquency rates are higher in two-parent than in one-parent homes. In fact, socioeconomic factors cannot by themselves produce the variations in delinquency rates that I observed. Racial differences in delinquency rates direct our attention to the structure of our society. Within our society we have a dominant group that writes and enforces laws and many alienated groups that produce the

majority of delinquents. We must control delinquency by reducing the alienation of these groups.

In addition to my own work, I have cited many other studies
to confirm and reinforce this interpretation. But I believe that
my interpretation is confirmed, in the last analysis, by our utter
failure to control delinquency with measures directed at delinquents.

A new attack on the problem of delinquency must use both
short-range and long-range methods. The short-range methods
can be directed primarily toward adolescents, but they must be
directed at groups, not at individuals. Our highest priority is
the group with the highest risk of delinquency. This group is
composed of adolescent Negro boys.

Delinquency control among Negroes must be carried out in
the frame of the Negro revolution, which is the single most important domestic issue facing our country in this century. Negro
youths, in their attitudes toward the police and toward other
authority, reflect the attitudes of Negro adults and of the Negro
subculture in general. Chief among the tensions and hostilities
that characterize the Negro subculture are those directed at the
police. These tensions and hostilities are summed up in the out-
cry against "police brutality," but as R. Blauner has pointed
out, Negroes are referring to more than physical violence. Negroes who talk of police brutality are also thinking of "the subtle
attack on personal dignity that manifests itself in unexplainable
questions and searches, in hostile and insolent attitudes toward
groups of young Negroes on the streets, or in cars, and in the
use of disrespectful and sometimes racist language" (Blauner,
1966, p. 6).

It does no good to try to assign blame for the lack of understanding between Negroes and the police. Regardless of whether
it is due primarily to the way that Negroes act toward policemen or to the way that policemen act toward Negroes, we must
start with the situation as it exists. Negro gang boys feel in their
relations with the police that they are always under the handicap
of being viewed as "suspicious characters," and Negro adults
and children in a ghetto see the police as an alien army of occu-

pation. A Harvard psychiatrist has described the effect this situation has on Negro children. Speaking of an eight-year-old boy, he reports:

> I have asked him to draw pictures—of himself, of his school, of his home, of anything he wishes. I get from him devastating portrayals: schools and homes that are as awful to see on paper as they are in real life; "outsiders" whose power and mercenary hostility are all too obvious; and everywhere, the police, looking for trouble, creating trouble, checking up, hauling people to court, calling them names, getting ready to hurt them, assault them, jail them, and beat them up—even if they are children [Coles, 1967, p. 104].

The primary responsibility to improve this image of police authority must rest with the government of our cities, but immediate action can be taken by the police. Five short-range methods can be used. These are the establishment of a citizens' review board, the institution of a police community-relations program, the relaxation of unnecessary restrictions, the use of detached workers in juvenile gangs, and the involvement of ghetto Negroes in police work.

After the riots in the Watts section of Los Angeles in 1965, newspapers contained much discussion of whether or not cities should establish citizens' boards to which cases of alleged brutality might be taken for review. The idea has merit, even though such boards would be incapable of handling either the subtle types of harassment described by Blauner or the basic attitude of suspicion toward Negro youth described by I. Piliavin and C. Werthman. Establishing such a board, in combination with other methods that will be described, might be taken by a ghetto population as an evidence of good faith. The board could serve as a demonstration of the impartiality of judicial processes, and in occasional instances it might redress individual grievances. But if other steps were not taken, the board would eventually cause additional mistrust and hostility—for example, if the board acquired the reputation of being dominated by whites or "Uncle Toms," or if it appeared to be a concession to pressure tactics rather than evidence of a real reform.

The same hazards are present in a police community-relations program. If the program achieves visible improvement in the actual behavior of policemen toward Negro citizens, it will be effective. If the program is concerned with improving the "image" of police and fails to alter their behavior, it will fail. Community relations are a two-way process. When a program is effective, citizens will see policemen in a new light, but policemen will also hold a better opinion of the citizens and will be less prone to engage in subtle types of harassment.

A fairly effective program has been in operation in San Francisco for several years. In San Francisco the Community Relations Unit consists of a small group of skilled officers, many of whom are Negroes. They work in plain clothes in areas of tension, trying to interpret the police viewpoint to the community and the community viewpoint to other members of the police department. Much of the unit's effectiveness came from the support it received from the chief of police and from the fact that knowledge of this support slowly spread within Negro ghettoes. The ABC lunch seminars described in Chapter III helped to demonstrate the backing for this program. On more than one occasion scores of young gang leaders heard the chief of police order that a specific incident be investigated or that a specific policy be changed. Precinct captains at these meetings not only heard first-hand accounts by gang boys who felt unjustly treated, but also observed the members of the Community Relations Unit discussing the situation with the boys. These meetings often were hostile, but they provided both an outlet for the hostility and a redress of some of the boys' legitimate grievances.

The next method I want to suggest for decreasing alienation, that of relaxing unnecessary restrictions on the activities of juveniles, should be combined with the use of detached workers in juvenile gangs. There are practical difficulties in relaxing restrictions on what is really a dangerous group of youths without providing an alternate measure of control. The purpose of many of the minor charges that comprise the bulk of police contacts with adolescents is to prevent more serious offenses. They can be viewed as part of a mechanism to keep adolescents under surveillance. The mechanism cannot be abandoned without providing a substitute.

Detached workers, who have been used in many cities (Merwin, 1960; Bernstein, 1964; Spergel, 1966), are agency representatives who operate within street gangs. They are generally able to divert gang members from extreme forms of illegal behavior such as gang fights, although they are less able to influence such individual acts as drug abuse. When an effective detached-worker program is in operation, it is possible to reduce police surveillance of the gang and even to abandon (by changing the law or by nonenforcement) those restrictions on juvenile activity, such as curfew and congregating laws, that are designed mainly to prevent crimes or to enforce compliance with cultural traditions. Abandonment of these restrictions would reduce the number of hostile contacts between juveniles and police.

An adequate number of detached workers, supported by their "lieutenants" and "aides" within the gangs and in high schools, can perform another function as well. Not only can they substitute for police surveillance and control of gang boys, but they can also function as a buffer between the police and juveniles. In San Francisco the streetworkers of Youth For Service have frequently proven their ability to prevent tense situations in the streets from exploding into violence. Often the police will stand back and watch while streetworkers reduce tension and disperse a crowd. The streetworkers have shown that it is generally possible to restore order without police intervention. Further, in the frequent situations in which gang boys are under suspicion (as, for example, when a group of boys are loitering on a street corner, where they may or may not be waiting for a bus), a streetworker can explain the situation to a policeman without arousing the hostility that would arise if the policeman himself approached the boys.

Detached workers provide a day-to-day surveillance and a form of delinquency prevention that makes it possible to reduce police activity. R. E. Rice and S. Adams (1965) have shown that gangs with detached workers require less conventional correctional activity than gangs without them. A detached-worker program thus allows a relaxation of the laws applying to juveniles. If most Negro gang boys were free of constant unpleasant contacts with policemen, it would be far easier for a community-relations unit to explain and emphasize the protection that the police give to citizens.

The last of the short-range measures to reduce police-juvenile hostility is to involve Negroes, including adolescent gang members, in police work. This measure is being tried in many cities, but I do not think it can now be carried out in Negro communities without simultaneously carrying out the other steps that have just been described. At the present time Negro gang boys who cooperate in such a program are regarded by their friends as having sold out to the enemy. Nevertheless, effective use of the other measures could relax tension to a point at which the program could be instituted. In addition to recruiting Negroes directly into the police force, the police department might invite boys as observers in patrol cars, so that they could see for themselves the problems policemen face. The police department might also hire police aides to carry out functions that do not require special skills. The more Negroes are actively involved in police work, the more they will be able to identify with and support the essential purpose of police work.

The long-range measures to reduce Negro delinquency are those which will enable Negroes to participate in the economic life of our society. No repressive measures will eliminate the hustler. Hustlers can only take up legitimate work if jobs are available. In order to make jobs available, the men and boys of the Negro community must receive training to qualify them for the jobs, the jobs must be located or created, and the restrictions that prevent high-school dropouts with police records from obtaining employment must be eliminated or circumvented.

Many difficulties stand in the way of recruiting gang boys for job training. A boy must be recruited at a time when he is unsuccessful at his hustle or when some crisis in his life has for the time being increased his desire for this training. Usually the recruiting effort must be aimed at teaching him "how to hustle in the world of work" rather than "how to give up the hustle." The trickster way of life is so deeply ingrained in these boys that they cannot conceive of any other.

Training these boys is difficult, too. Experience in federal programs such as the Neighborhood Youth Corps and Job

Corps (Purcell, 1966) has shown that when the recruiting effort has really reached the "hard core" gang boys, the programs must deal with their suspicion and resentment of authority. These boys are exceptionally prone to take offense and must be supervised by men who understand their attitude. Gang boys tend to use their free time in the ways they learned in the streets of their home neighborhoods, and these ways present problems to communities near job corps camps (Caesar, 1966). Nevertheless, skilled instructors and counselors in many camps have already helped boys to qualify themselves for work in various semiskilled occupations.

The crucial point in work-training programs for gang boys is job placement. No amount of counseling can convince them that training is worthwhile unless they see that other boys have used it to obtain real jobs. Job placement is difficult because many employers refuse to take a chance with these boys. Work-training programs need personnel specifically assigned to job development, who will find vacant positions and convince personnel managers that the training program is turning out workers who can fill them. When a position is found, counseling is often necessary to persuade a boy to apply for the job and to help him to do so. Even after a boy is placed, he often needs continued counseling to help him remain on the job.

Therefore a work-training program must be divided into two difficult tasks, both essential. The first task is to train the boy. The second task, job development, is to train the community to accept these boys into economically productive work (King, 1967, p. 197).

If we believe that we should direct gang boys into the productive community, we need to change our economic system to provide room for them. One major change is the "New Careers for the Poor" concept (Pearl and Riessman, 1965), which suggests that we should be prepared to train people on the job rather than require that they be able to function as soon as they are hired. If the "New Careers" concept were generally accepted, it would do much to reduce delinquency.

Job training is aimed at the identity crisis of adolescence. Its purpose is to show a boy that he is the type of person who can support himself by work. A program that moves him through training into a job is the best way to do this, but another (although less effective) way is the voluntary work project (Amos, Manella, and Southwell, 1965, Chs. 6, 8, 12). In San Francisco, Youth For Service has found that voluntary projects are an excellent means of attracting boys to the agency and instilling attitudes that lead them into more formal training. The visible accomplishments of these projects have also helped to modify community attitudes towards the youths. The voluntary projects are supervised by streetworkers, who recruit the boys, transport them to the work site, provide tools, arrange for lunch, and return the boys home in the evening.

Job training for these boys serves the same function that schools serve for many children. Basically our schools are our primary method of acculturation of children, and they should play a central role in long-range delinquency prevention. Central city schools, however, have failed street gang boys. This is evidenced not only by the boys' high dropout rates, but by their low scores on tests of academic achievement. It is not unusual for these boys to have test scores two to four years below their actual grade placement. Educational reform will not be discussed in this book. W. E. Amos (1967) has written an excellent summary of the schools' role in delinquency control. If schools are to serve gang boys, they must adapt themselves to the students, for it has become obvious that the boys will not change themselves to conform to the schools. But it is unrealistic to believe that the schools, no matter how they are improved, can serve the needs of everyone. The alternate routes to success that are now available to a few boys, such as federal job-training programs and union apprenticeship training, must be expanded greatly if we are to bring the alienated lower-class Negroes into the mainstream of our society. These alternate routes will undoubtedly be necessary for generations.

Even while we are taking steps to combat the delinquency of lower-class Negro boys, we must not forget that these boys are only a small part of the total problem of delinquency. Measures that will reduce delinquency among Negro gang boys will simultaneously be effective for Spanish-speaking, Oriental,

Caucasian, and other groups of street gang boys. They will not be effective for the middle-class boys who make up a large portion of our labeled delinquents and an even larger portion of unlabeled delinquents. The most effective measure against middle-class delinquency, it appears to me, is to do what these youths themselves have asked of us: to admit them to participation in adult life. The methods we need to use for alienated middle-class adolescents include breaking down the age barriers in our society, setting up mechanisms whereby youth can make important decisions for themselves, and providing alternative pathways to success. Only the second of these will be easy.

I know of no mechanism whereby an agency or a group of dedicated citizens can break down all of the age-segregation barriers imposed on children by adults. Individuals can help to do this by accepting the adolescent sons and daughters of their friends and neighbors into social gatherings (especially when they can be included without their parents) or by providing opportunities for them to work. I am not suggesting that parents need to spend more time with their children. Adolescence is a time when role models must be found outside of the family. The types of contact I am suggesting are those in which the adolescent is accepted into a group of adults as an individual in his own right, not as an appendage of his parents.

The use of adolescents for unskilled jobs in small businesses would give them opportunities to associate with adults. One of the most important barriers to this type of employment is the laws and regulations governing child labor, social security, unemployment compensation, and workmen's compensation. The amount of paper work required for each employee is so great that it effectively prohibits informal short-term employment. Two other barriers are compulsory school attendance and the draft. At present, when a boy reaches the age at which he is allowed to leave school, he finds that he is faced with the choice of remaining in school as a full-time student or of being drafted into military service. Either alternative precludes gainful employment.

Age barriers can be broken down in other ways. One is institutional: to provide opportunities for children and adolescents to work and play with each other. The sandlot baseball of my childhood, in contrast to the modern Little League, provided the mechanism of "choosing up sides," which allowed children of different sizes and abilities to play on the same team. A small child was of little value to his team, but was accepted nevertheless by older boys. There are many opportunities to bring adolescents and children together in recreation programs—and in education, where older children can be used to teach younger ones (Lippitt and Lohman, 1965).

Although we cannot easily break down the segregation of adolescents from adults, we can readily provide opportunities for adolescents to participate in decision-making. All the suggestions of the adolescents who attended the governor's conference reported in Chapter IV give ways of doing this. Not a single one of the ten recommendations is impractical; every one could be implemented by a few policy-making adults. The University of California's School of Criminology is giving adolescents opportunities for decision-making in a federally financed experimental project to reduce middle-class delinquency (Lohman and Carter, 1966). Two middle-class suburban communities were selected for this project. In both communities a youth council was set up to organize and run activities for teen-age boys. These councils, consisting of approximately equal numbers of adults and adolescents with equal voting rights and equal privileges, have succeeded in starting successful projects involving teen-agers, such as a motorcycle club for adolescents and adults, an automobile repair center, and a teen-age recreation center. More important, the involvement of adolescents and adults in joint activities has had an important effect in redefining the attitudes of both groups. As the experimental project continues, adults are more and more able to perceive the adolescents' activities as legitimate rather than as delinquent. Although the project has already given many adolescents a sense of participation in community life, it has not completely succeeded in breaking down age separation in the communities. Adults still see most of the activities as concerns of teen-agers rather than of the community.

I know of no projects in the United States (except vocational training in a few schools) that have addressed themselves to the middle-class problem of the lack of alternative pathways to success. In Europe many countries have an educational system that separates young adolescents into two courses of learning. Some go into an academic course leading to the universities, and the remainder go into a system of apprenticeships leading to labor and commercial skills. The system of apprenticeships does not do justice to children whose abilities develop late or to those who have temporary difficulties in childhood. Nevertheless, the programs discussed earlier that are aimed at lower-class boys, such as the Job Corps and union apprenticeships, might be developed into alternate pathways for middle-class youth also. At present they are not designed for, nor in the case of the federal programs are they even available to, middle-class youth.

One obvious alternative to school would be military service if this alternative were acceptable to our youth. The United States is now fighting an unpopular war, and to many of our youth military service represents the ultimate degree of surrender to a society that allows them no choice. If we were at peace, military service could again become voluntary. Should this happen, it could again be an alternate pathway from adolescence into manhood.

I have confined my discussion of delinquency prevention to measures aimed at boys. Delinquency prevention for girls is also important, but not as urgent. In general, measures that keep boys out of trouble will also help girls, although effective and worthwhile programs for girls can also be developed. Much of the visible delinquency of girls is sexual misbehavior. Early sex education and family-planning programs may reduce promiscuity and teen-age pregnancy, but I believe that undesirable sexual activity of both boys and girls is primarily a symptom of the alienation of youth and of the need to assume adult status. Preventive efforts should be directed at this alienation.

In the last analysis, delinquency prevention must develop out of an improvement of our ability to live with adolescents. Many types of behavior can be handled by informal mechanisms that do not result in a delinquency label. The greater a community's ability to "absorb" delinquency (Lohman and Carter, 1966), the less alienation will be forced onto the youth of the community, and the less they will find it necessary to seek satisfaction of their needs in ways which damage the community. We have reached our present alarming level of delinquency labeling by following this circle in the opposite direction: The more a community must resort to formal processes to control the behavior of its youth, the more boys and girls will be permanently alienated, and the more they will resort to antisocial activity to fulfill their psychological needs. It is time to try to reverse the cycle.

We cannot control delinquency by addressing ourselves to the delinquent. The delinquency problem in modern society is one result of the structure of the society itself. Its control requires changes in our economic system and our education system. To make these changes, adults must alter their attitude toward young people. Our choice is to accept them into our society or to allow them to become delinquents.

• 2 • PUNISHMENT, REHABILITATION, AND REFORM

When John Snow removed the handle from a community water pump in London, he made a dramatic gesture demonstrating that cholera could be controlled. A plaque in Broad Street still commemorates the event. But there is no proof that his action stopped the cholera epidemic, and indeed the removal of a single source of infection in so large a city could hardly have prevented more than a few cases. Nevertheless, Dr. Snow succeeded in conquering cholera. His demonstration that water transmitted the disease was the foundation of public-health measures that have since brought cholera under effective control. Filtration and chlorination of water controlled cholera, and although it still exists, in our modern world it has become a rarity.

My studies, like Dr. Snow's, were epidemiological. Like his, mine will be of use only if they lead in some way to the control of the condition under study. Delinquency resembles cholera in the necessity for community-wide rather than individual control methods, and delinquency control requires that we change our methods of socializing our children rather than treat individual delinquents or small groups of delinquents.

Measures for combating delinquency can be divided into punishment of individual delinquents, rehabilitation of delinquents or predelinquents, and changes in the environment that produces delinquency. Most of the long-range measures described in the previous chapter are directed at the environment. Both punishment and rehabilitation have a place in delinquency control, and it is not suggested that we abandon them. Nevertheless, I believe that we have overused punishment in the past and should now restrict its use and that we must undertake rehabilitation with a new viewpoint before we can do it successfully.

We can no more abandon punishment of delinquents than we can abandon the medical treatment of a patient who has contracted cholera. But punishment is an effective measure of social control only when it is applied to a small proportion of the population. If too many people are punished, the result can be rebellion. If only a few people who have committed the worst offenses are punished, others will be deterred from similar offenses. In an ideal situation, delinquency labeling should become what K. T. Erikson (1964, pp. 13–14) has called a "boundary maintaining mechanism." In his view, the interactions of members of a society with law-enforcement officers serve as a visible reminder to other members of the society of the limits of permissible conduct in that society. These interactions serve to "mark the outside limits of the area within which the norm has jurisdiction, and in this way assert how much diversity and variability can be contained within the system before it begins to lose its distinct structure, its cultural integrity."

Our present juvenile-delinquency problem stems from our cultural intolerance of diversity and variability. Our boundaries are far too restrictive. In our effort to maintain our ideal culture we have excluded from that culture most Negroes and all adolescents who are not in school. Our culture (which we like to believe consists of men and women who work, keep house, and raise their children) also has no room for the unemployed, for the immature, for the inefficient, or for other deviants. To preserve our image of American life we have adopted a variety of methods for isolating those individuals who do not conform to our ideal. Thus Negroes are isolated in ghettoes, adolescents in schools, and incompetents in mental hospitals or prisons. Even though these groups together probably comprise more than half of our population, once they have been isolated their plight can be ignored. It usually is.

We belong to a pluralistic culture that we persist in treating as uniform. Our laws are made by only one segment of this culture, but in our cities we find other elements for whom many of the laws are unnecessarily restrictive. As a result, we have alienated large groups of people, and we have applied a delinquency label to many of them. Our high rates of delinquency are evidence that our boundary-maintaining mechanism has excluded too many adolescents. The solution is to integrate the diverse elements into our society rather than to punish them ever more severely for being outside.

The high delinquency rates that have been documented show that our present boundary-maintaining mechanism no longer protects the integrity of our culture; it has become one of the forces of disintegration. Our narrow definition of acceptable behavior can hardly be satisfied by a normal teen-age boy in a city. This statement can be illustrated by examples taken from Appendix A, which gives the offenses for which a boy could be arrested in San Francisco in 1960. (The list is not much different today although the "congregating" law is no longer in force, and it is not much different in any urban area in the United States.) A boy who was not in his home or at school could be arrested for playing ball in the street, exploding a firecracker, shooting a BB gun, lighting a fire, gambling, throwing paper in the street, writing on a wall, penciling a mustache on a billboard, engaging in a fight, bullying another boy, swearing, or possessing liquor. Moreover, he could not join a group of more than three other boys, loiter on a corner, or be on the street late at night. In school, he could be arrested for a "behavior problem" and, at home, for refusing to obey his parents. Sexual relations (unless he were married) were illegal, and so was any other action which could be considered a "danger of immorality." It is hard to imagine just what he could do, besides go to school or engage in organized recreation.

The results of our restrictions on adolescents are seen not only in delinquency statistics—which show that a quarter to a third of the white seventeen-year-old boys in the middle-class areas of San Francisco were labeled as delinquents in 1960— but also in the development of "youth cultures." It is becoming increasingly difficult for young people to progress smoothly into adult society, and their response in many instances has been to form a society of their own. More and more, youth cultures appear to be rejecting the entire value system of the middle-class adult world. This rejection is not due simply to the psychological necessity for a rebellion in adolescence. Normal developmental patterns require an adolescent rebellion directed at parents, but not one directed at our entire cultural pattern. Our adolescents are rejecting our society mainly because our society has already rejected them.

The best answer to the development of a youth culture is not to punish the rebellious youth; it is to find a place for them in the conventional world where they can achieve a measure of self-fulfillment. This place should be in productive activity, and it should be in a place where they associate with adults.

But the alienation of large numbers of white middle-class adolescents is not the most important point that emerges from an epidemiological study of delinquency. The high delinquency rates found for Negro boys are a symptom of the crisis among Negroes that could destroy our entire society. Our housing patterns have hidden the crisis from the view of white Americans: Since World War II the white middle class has withdrawn from city to suburb and the central areas of most of our cities have been left to become Negro ghettoes. In these ghettoes Negroes are physically separated from the majority of whites, who remain ignorant of the poverty and lack of opportunity in Black America. In San Francisco I found that most Negro boys are delinquent. The delinquency rates that I found in 1960 and 1964 do much to explain both the Hunters Point riot of 1966 and Negro riots in many other cities: A group of youth who feel that they have been rejected by our society have now decided that their best opportunity is to attack the society itself.

The problem of delinquency control among Negroes is closely related to the problem of riot control in urban ghettoes. The same alienation from society is at the root of both problems. It is possible to suppress riots by force, and it is possible (although impractical) to imprison all delinquents. But to do so will only postpone trouble; it will not cure it. A cure for the alienation of Negroes must be sought in other ways. The delinquency control methods that I have described can be effective only if Negroes begin to feel themselves a part of American society. They cannot do so as long as we restrict their activities and punish them for minor deviations. We must now search for ways to reduce the number of youth whom we punish, by reserving punishment for truly antisocial forms of conduct, by providing nonpunitive methods of social control, and by giving adolescents opportunities to work.

Present methods of rehabilitation can no more control delinquency than can punishment. Unlike punishment, their failure has not been due to overuse, and rehabilitation is an important objective in any delinquency control program. Our failure to rehabilitate delinquents stems primarily from our concept of the delinquent as a deviant. Although it is true that many delinquents are mentally ill, the evidence I have cited does not permit us to say that *most* delinquents should be treated by pediatricians, psychiatrists, or other healers. I have already discussed my conviction that the role of medicine and psychiatry in delinquency control should be that of preventing children from being labeled as delinquents if their behavior is due to disease.

Nevertheless, as long as we have delinquents, we face the necessity of rehabilitation in a broader sense. The rehabilitation that should be a part of delinquency control consists of those measures that enable a labeled delinquent to find a suitable place in adult society. To carry out these measures, we must first reduce the overwhelming caseloads of rehabilitation workers. When we have done so, we must approach the problem from the point of view that delinquents are for the most part reacting normally to the world in which they find themselves.

Rehabilitation must consist of measures to give delinquents an opportunity to enter a different world.

Counseling of delinquents and predelinquents in the past has largely failed to provide this opportunity. Counseling, which includes such methods as psychotherapy, social casework, or Big Brother programs, generally starts with the aim of effecting a change in the delinquent (or predelinquent) himself. Even employment counseling often takes this form. Although it is true that successful rehabilitation requires a change in the delinquent, it cannot start with an attempt to change him. Rehabilitation must begin by finding a place for him, and then proceed to make it possible for him to move into that place. It does no good to motivate a high-school dropout to seek employment, unless there is a job opening for him.

Rehabilitation counseling for most delinquents must start with jobs. It is no easy task to prepare a street gang member for a job, but in my experience it is even more difficult to prepare a job for him. A pressing need in most job-training programs is for personnel who can work in the community to find employers who will hire adolescents and who will accept them despite barriers of race, police records, and lack of education. If jobs were available for delinquents, the rehabilitation of an individual delinquent could proceed like a job-training program and indeed with the same personnel.

Along with job development and training, rehabilitation must include the traditional counseling methods that have been used in the past. But the emphasis and direction of the counseling could be different. Instead of directing a delinquent away from certain activities, he could be directed toward those activities that would aid him in his identity crisis by helping him to form an acceptable self-image.

Our primary reliance in delinquency control cannot, of course, be rehabilitation of delinquents. The number of delinquents is already far too large to permit such reliance, and the number will probably grow even larger unless we find effective ways of prevention. The delinquency prevention methods that I believe we should adopt are described in section 1 of this chapter. Adoption of these methods would reduce the number of adjudicated delinquents and thus permit more effective rehabilitation of the remainder.

Control of delinquency must start with a change in our way of bringing up children. I have pointed to features of our society that are actively driving our youth into antisocial forms of behavior. By not allowing adolescents to participate in our society we have isolated them in worlds of their own. To bring them back into our society, we need to decide anew what behavior we are prepared to tolerate and what behavior must be controlled. When we have expanded our limits of tolerable behavior, we can consider for each type of intolerable behavior whether the best method of control is to be formal—by labeling the offender as a delinquent—or informal, which means finding nonlegal and nonpunitive means of preventing repetition.

The intolerance that is a basic feature of our society will not be easy to remedy. Intolerance of Negroes has been a characteristic of the United States for centuries, and it has resulted in our present high rates of delinquency of Negro boys. Control of Negro delinquency requires us to admit Negroes to full participation in our society. Negroes, who have lived in the United States since its founding, have not only a legal but also a moral right to first-class citizenship. Although we cannot *give* this to them, we can remove the discriminatory barriers that exclude them. One barrier is economic. Until Negroes have the same opportunities as other citizens, we discriminate when we demand of them the standards of behavior and performance we expect of those for whom the opportunities are real. Another barrier is the one to which I have addressed myself in this book, our definition of unacceptable behavior.

Intolerance of adolescents is a newer phenomenon than intolerance of Negroes. It is rooted in our modern economic system in which children have become a liability and no longer an asset and in which mechanization is constantly reducing the need for unskilled workers. In the past, adolescents were accepted into the adult world; in fact, it is only in very recent years that adolescence has been considered as a stage of life distinct from childhood and adulthood (Ariès, 1965, p. 29).

Measures are already in operation on a small scale to help

bring adolescents back into the adult world. These measures can, in the long run, reduce alienation and delinquency. The reduction will not be easy, nor will we see rapid results. Juvenile delinquency arises from defects in our patterns of living together and of bringing up children. A solution requires reforming these patterns before reforming our delinquent children.

APPENDIX A: OFFENSE CATEGORIES USED BY SAN FRANCISCO POLICE DEPARTMENT AND JUVENILE COURT IN 1960 AND 1964

(Italicized categories were coded on 1960 data cards. Suspicion of an offense was coded under the appropriate offense category.)

1. *Homicide*
   Murder
   Manslaughter

2. *Robbery*
   Armed
   Other

3. *Assault*
   Assault to murder
   Assault with deadly weapon
   Assault, other. Battery
   (Note: Assault to rape is classified under sex offenses.)

4. *Auto Theft*
   Vehicle theft, joyride
   Driving or taking car or other vehicle without owner's consent
   Accomplice to such an act

5. *Theft*

    Larceny and theft (except auto)
    Auto tampering
    Car clouting, boosting
    Purse snatching
    Petty theft
    Illegal collection for newspapers

6. *Burglary*

    Burglary
    Receiving or selling stolen property
    Forgery and checks

7. *Sex Offenses*

    Rape (forcible, statutory)
    Assault to rape, and attempt
    Illegitimate sexual relations
    Danger of immorality
    Prostitution, pandering
    Contributing to delinquency of minor
    Bigamy, incest
    Pregnant (unmarried)
    Homosexual acts or tendencies
    Impersonating opposite sex
    Indecent exposure
    Molesting infant
    Other sex delinquencies

8. *Narcotics*

    Use or possession

9. *Other Offenses*

    Possession of weapons
    Desertion of their children by juveniles
    Failure to provide
    Drunk driving
    Hit and run, failure to render aid

Arson
Escape (Youth Authority facility, jail, mental institution),
    aiding in escape
Kidnapping
Extortion
Violation of immigration or import regulations
Destroying property with explosives
AWOL, armed forces
Destruction of railroad property
Sheltering felons
Violation of fish or game laws
Unlawful discharge of firearms
Defrauding innkeeper
Exploding firecrackers
Shooting BB gun
Playing ball in street
Obscene photos, letters
Burning without permit
Gambling
Litterbug
Causing false arrest
Outraging public decency

10. *Delinquent Tendencies*

Incorrigible, runaway, beyond control of parents
Malicious mischief
Insubordination, refuses to obey
Behavior problem in school
Minor destruction of property, defacing property
    (vandalism)
False fire alarms
Resisting an officer
Truancy
Signing parent's name to absentee slip
Glue or gasoline sniffing
Disorderly conduct, disturbing the peace
Fighting
Bullying younger children

Obscene language or phone calls
Drunkenness or drinking
Possession of liquor
Vagrancy, late hours (curfew)
Loitering, prowling, trespassing, "Peeping Tom"
Crashing the theater
Evading payment on public carrier
Congregating (not illegal in 1964)
Failure to adjust or obey court order

APPENDIX B: STUDY METHODOLOGY

I. THE DELINQUENT POPULATION

The basic data for the study were two decks of IBM cards, prepared by the Research and Statistics Subcommittee of the San Francisco Committee on Youth. The author became a member of the subcommittee in 1963 and, after the first subcommittee report was prepared, was given permission to make further studies of the data, aided by a grant from the School of Public Health of the University of California at Berkeley.

The two decks of IBM cards were prepared in 1961 and 1965 by juvenile court and police-department staff members, under the supervision of members of the subcommittee, from original court and police-department records. They contained the name and census tract of residence of the delinquent, the name of the offense charged, the disposition, and basic demographic data. For the cases seen in juvenile court these demographic data included age, sex, race, income, data on family composition, and some other data, such as religion, which was not used in the present study. The police contact cards contained less demographic information, because it was obviously impossible to investigate such cases as thoroughly as do court officials. The major information that was missing on the reports of police contacts was the family income and the family composition of the delinquent.

It proved necessary to eliminate a large number of errors in the IBM cards. Despite the care taken in the original coding, a variety of random and systematic errors had appeared. The most important of these errors concerned the census tract of residence. All of the police contact cards were eventually recoded by the author, as a sizeable number of cards had been coded to show the census tract where the contact had been made rather than that in which the juvenile lived. This recoding allowed a check of other items on the police records: The most important of the other errors were some random errors in age and race of the delinquent and occasional errors in the spelling of names.

The cards prepared for juvenile-court cases had been coded more accurately. In 1964, when the cards were recoded, many of the original records had been removed from file and destroyed. It was possible to check the remaining records, however; the only important discrepancy found in this group was that census-tract coding used the tracts as they were defined in 1950 rather than the 1960 division. For this reason the 1950 tracts were used throughout the study.

A major difficulty appeared for the 1960 juvenile-court cases. At the start of 1960, family income was recorded only for "official cases" in the juvenile court, that is, cases in which a petition had been filed. From July of that year, income data were recorded for all cases. Thus, family income was recorded as "unknown" for approximately half of the unofficial juvenile-court cases. This problem was handled by assuming that the distribution of incomes for the first six months of the year was similar to the distribution for the second six months. For each tabulation of income during the analysis of the data, a proportionate assignment of these cases was made into income categories according to the income distribution of the unofficial cases seen during the latter half of the year. It is believed that this procedure did not result in any great error.

Once the coding errors had been eliminated, an unduplicated list was made of all the individuals whose names had been recorded. For this procedure individuals were identified by name, age, race, and census tract of residence. When an individual delinquent appeared more than once, he was assigned to the most serious administrative or offense category in which he appeared. It was assumed that a juvenile-court citation implied a more serious offense than a police-department "warning" and that an official juvenile-court record represented a more serious offense than did an unofficial record. If a case appeared more than once in the same administrative category, it was coded into the most serious offense category, on the basis that a named offense was more serious than a coding of "delinquent tendencies" or "other offenses" and that offenses against persons were more serious than offenses against property. No ambiguities were found during this operation. It was possible to check the final list of delinquents with the similar list made for the original subcommittee report. Only minor discrepancies were found.

Age limits of 8 to 17 were set for the study population. The lower limit was set because of the small number of cases aged 5 to 7. There were only 14 such cases in 1960. A check of the original police-department files showed that 90 percent of the cases coded as age 17–19 were actually 17 years old. Fortunately, the IBM cards coded for unofficial juvenile-court cases for the first half of 1960 coded single years of age instead of the coding into three-year categories used for all the other cards. This coding made possible a similar check of this category of juvenile-court cases, which showed that 89 percent of the 17–19-year olds recorded were 17 years of age. It was assumed that the same ratio applied to the official juvenile-court cases. In 1960 there were 16 offenders 20 years of age who were seen in juvenile court or recorded by the police department. These 16 juveniles were excluded from the study. Because it was not possible to eliminate all of the cards of 18- and 19-year-olds, the problem was handled in a manner similar to that for the deficiencies in income data referred to above: For each tabulation by age, the number of 17–19-year-olds was reduced by 10 percent, and the resulting number was assumed to represent 17-year-olds.

The racial categories of "white," "Mexican," "Negro," and "Other" were redefined into "white," "white-Spanish," "Negro,"

"Chinese," and "Other." This redefinition was accomplished by coding surnames of delinquents who had originally been classified "white" according to whether or not they were of Spanish derivation and by coding surnames of delinquents who had originally been classified "other race" according to whether or not they were of Chinese derivation. The final categories were defined as follows:

White: Coded on records as white, surname not Spanish

White-Spanish: Coded on records as white, surname Spanish *or* coded on records as Mexican.

Negro: Coded on records as Negro.

Chinese: Coded on records as "other race," surname Chinese.

Other: The residual group. An attempt was made to separate out a Japanese group, but the number of Japanese delinquents proved to be too small to analyze, and the Japanese delinquents were eventually included as "other." In addition to Japanese, the main racial components of the "other" group were Filipinos, Samoans, and American Indians.

Delinquents who lived outside of San Francisco were excluded from the study. Delinquents in census tract K-1 were also excluded. This census tract contains a portion of the city proper, but also a large offshore naval base with several thousand 17-year-old enlisted men who were not exposed to the risk of being recorded as delinquent in San Francisco. In addition, two large parks, census areas F and I, were left out of the tabulations.

The 1964 data were handled in a manner similar to the 1960 data, but with far less difficulty. Experience gained in correcting the 1960 cards was used to improve the coding procedure in 1964, and it was not necessary to recode any of the cards in 1964, nor were any income or age assumptions necessary.

II. THE POPULATION AT RISK

Basic data for the 1960 population at risk was obtained directly from the 1960 census (U.S. Census, Census Tracts, 1960).

Certain estimates were necessary, however, to make the categories compatible. The categories chosen for the study were sex, age, race, income, number of parents with whom the juvenile was living, and geographical area. No assumptions were necessary for the category of sex, but none of the others proved completely compatible.

To make age categories compatible for the delinquent population and the population at risk, it was necessary to convert the census five-year groupings to the three-year categories into which the delinquents' age had been grouped and to make a one-year grouping for seventeen-year-olds. This was accomplished by assigning one-fifth of each census five-year group to each single year of age and recombining into the desired categories.

The detailed breakdowns found in the census data had been made separately for the white population and the nonwhite. In addition, some breakdowns were given for the population of "White with Spanish Surname." This last category did not contain information on number of parents with whom children were living.

In order to form racial categories similar to those used for the delinquent population, a "White" group was obtained by subtracting the "White with Spanish Surname" from the census category "White." The "White with Spanish Surname" category was considered equivalent to the delinquent "White-Spanish" category. To divide the census "Nonwhite" category into Negro, Chinese, Japanese, and other groups, San Francisco birth registration data were used. The nonwhite group in each census area was divided into these categories in proportion to the number of births of each category in each census area in 1960. This procedure was checked by comparing the proportion of Negroes to all nonwhites in each census area.

Census data give family income, not individual income. It was necessary to assume that, in each income category, the number of children was proportional to the number of families. This assumption is obviously not correct, and it introduced an uncorrectable bias into the income tabulations. A similar assumption was necessary for the categorization of the number of parents with whom a juvenile was living, a grouping that for the sake of convenience will be called "living arrangement." This category was considered to include both stepparents and adoptive parents. The number of white and nonwhite children under eighteen and the number of them living with two parents were obtained directly from the census. The number not living with either parent was calculated from the item giving the number of children of heads of households living in households. It was necessary to assume that the number of children from eight to seventeen years old with a given living arrangement was proportional to the total of all children with that living arrangement up to seventeen years old and that the proportions for white and nonwhite were applicable to each of the white or nonwhite races included. These assumptions are also not correct and were used only for the preliminary tabulations.

It is not known whether juvenile-court officials recorded as "family income" the total income available to the family or the income of the chief wage earner in the family. It is also unknown to what extent families of delinquents tend to overstate or understate their incomes. This information was recorded by individual probation officers, who may have used different methods of acquiring the information. It would be expected that any bias resulting from these errors, if they exist, would be toward overstating the number of delinquents from low-income families, thus increasing the apparent delinquency rates at low levels of income.

The assumption that the number of children at a given income level is proportional to the number of families at that level can be examined from other census data. A comparison by income level of the number of persons of all ages in California in families of two or more with the percentage of families at each level (U.S. Census, 1962, Table 6) is available. From these comparisons it is possible to estimate that the method chosen resulted in a 15 to 20 percent overestimate of the number of children in the lowest-income grouping of the population at risk (despite the prevailing impression that these families have more children than families of higher income). The bias from this error would be in the opposite direction from the former one, as it would result in an apparently lower delinquency rate for the lowest-income group. It is believed that the combination of biases is insufficient to have caused the differences in delinquency rates by income that are reported in Chapter V and that these are essentially correct.

Because no census figures were available for the population at risk in 1964, estimates were prepared. It later proved possible to check the author's estimates by comparing them with similar estimates, prepared in 1966 by the San Francisco Department of City Planning. The two estimates were very similar. The author's estimates were made by the Composite Method of D. J. Bogue and B. Duncan (1959) and have been published elsewhere (Eisner, 1965). This method uses school attendance as an indicator of changes in the population aged 5–14, and both school attendance by, and births to, women aged 15–19 to estimate the 15–19 population. The estimate includes a breakdown by age, sex, and color (white and nonwhite). In order to be able to examine the data by geographical area, the estimated population was also divided between an eastern and a western area. This procedure was followed separately for each sex and color by assuming that the relative changes in the juvenile population paralleled changes in the number of births of each color in each area. A crude estimate was made for each area, then the crude estimates were adjusted proportionately to the previously estimated totals for the entire city.

III. SIGNIFICANCE TESTS

Significance of differences between adjusted rates was calculated by summing the variance ($V = pq\,N^2/n$) for each cell and computing a standard error for each adjusted rate ($S^2 = \Sigma V/[\Sigma N]^2$). Results are expressed as "highly significant" when significant at the 1 percent level and "significant" when significant at the 5 percent level.

IV. SELECTION OF AREAS FOR SPECIAL COMPARISONS

The two racial-comparison areas in section 2 of Chapter III were selected on the basis of having racially mixed populations in which the nonwhite populations were predominantly of one race. This purpose was accomplished by including in each comparison area those census tracts in which the total population was 20 to 80 percent white and in which, in one area, the nonwhite population was at least 80 percent Negro and, in the other area, at least 80 percent Chinese. The Negro-white comparison area comprised 17 noncontiguous census tracts; the Chinese-white comparison area included 7 contiguous tracts.

The comparison areas used to study family structure (section 3) did not have to have racially mixed populations, but it was felt advisable to limit them to tracts with a minimum nonwhite population of 1000. The Negro area for this comparison included 15 noncontiguous tracts, and the Chinese area included 12 contiguous ones.

For the area analysis, it was felt necessary to use as many tracts as possible, and the requirements were eased. A population of 300 nonwhite children under 18 was decided upon as a minimum requirement. This decision made possible the use of the same 12 tracts for the Chinese area. All of these tracts had a nonwhite population that was at least 90 percent Chinese. A total of 45 tracts met the population criterion: in 16, the nonwhite population was at least 80 percent Negro and in 6 others it was 60 to 80 percent Negro. All 22 of these tracts were chosen for the Negro area. The white areas were chosen to include all census tracts with at least 500 white children under 18, and the "Total" area included all tracts that had at least 500 children of any race. The white area comprised 75 tracts, and the "Total" area 96.

The "Eastern" and "Western" areas used in section 5 were selected on the basis of dividing the city according to a subjectively determined social-class basis. Census areas generally regarded as middle-class were grouped together, as were census areas generally regarded as lower-class or mixed middle- and lower-class. This grouping resulted in a division of the city into approximately equal halves along an irregular line from north to south.

V. FACTOR ANALYSIS. (This portion of the study was designed and carried out by Dr. Harley B. Messinger, who wrote the following description.)

Two analyses were run: a combined data analysis, and a single-race-data analysis. The combined-data analysis used indices derived from the 96 (out of 118) San Francisco census tracts that had a population of at least 500 children under 18.

The following criteria were used to select single-race tracts:

1. White Tracts. Population of at least 500 white children under 18.
   Seventy-five tracts met this criterion.
2. Negro Tracts. Population of at least 300 nonwhite children under 18. At least 60 percent of the nonwhite population Negro.
   Forty-five tracts met the first criterion, and 22 of these also met the second. Sixteen of the 22 tracts had a nonwhite population that was at least 80 percent Negro.
3. Chinese Tracts. Population of at least 300 nonwhite children under 18. At least 60 percent of the nonwhite population Chinese.
   Twelve tracts met both criteria. In all of them the nonwhite population was over 90 percent Chinese.
4. Tracts that had less than the required white or nonwhite populations and tracts in which no single nonwhite race amounted to 60 percent of the total were excluded from the study.

Thus, a total of 109 census tracts were included in the single-race data.

A total of 13 area indices were derived from census-tract data and health-department statistics, centering around the year 1960. These indices were used as independent variables. Definitions of them are given in Appendix D. Male delinquency and female delinquency were used as dependent variables. These delinquency rates were calculated as number of delinquents per 1,000 under 18 years of age (including juvenile-court cases and police-department "warned but not cited" cases).

Indices and delinquency rates were calculated in two ways. For the combined-data analysis, they were calculated for the entire population of each tract. For the single-race-data analysis, statistics were divided into those for the white population and those for the nonwhite population of each tract. An exception was the *integration* index, which referred to the total population of the tract in both analyses.

All variables were standardized by the T-score technique, which transformed them into deviates of normal distributions with means of 50 units and standard deviations of 10 units.

A preliminary multiple-regression analysis showed many interactions among the standardized variables. Because methods that analyze the correlation matrix as a whole may generate nonsense in the presence of interactions, the factor analysis of the independent variables was done by Tryon's method (Tryon and Bailey, 1966). This method starts by choosing as the pivot variable for the first cluster that variable with the greatest variation in the values of squared correlations with other variables. Variables are added according to their similarity to the pivot in correlation patterns using a modification of Burt's proportionality index. Usually four variables are enough to define a cluster, but more may be added if highly collinear (similar) candidates are available. The cluster is treated as a composite variable or factor. This factor is partialled out of the correlation matrix and the whole process repeated until at least 95 percent of the total communality (common variance) is accounted for by the derived factors.

The technique of spherical analysis was used to display the relationship of each variable to each factor and to other variables. Because any three orthogonal factors can be used as a coordinate system for a plot on a spherical surface, the variables were plotted on a spherical surface with a coordinate system defined by the three selected factors. The more highly correlated any two variables, the closer they will be on the plot; the higher the factor loading on a given variable, the nearer the variable will appear to the coordinate axis that the factor represents.

As a final step, the three factors derived from each area analysis of the original independent variables were used as new independent variables in a multiple-regression analysis, with male and female delinquency rates as dependent variables.

The results of the area analyses and the multiple regressions are given in Appendix D. They are also shown graphically in Figures 1 through 4, Chapter III.

Significance testing of the differences in observed and predicted mean delinquency rates in white, Negro, and Chinese tracts was done by analysis of variance and F tests. Multiple comparisons among the individual means were made by the S-method.

APPENDIX C: TABULATIONS OF POPULATIONS

Table C-1: Male Delinquent Population (1960) by Race and Variable Factors Studied

Variable Factors	White	White-Spanish	Negro	Chinese	Other	Total
All delinquents	2,692	525	1,190	81	162	4,650
Police dept. only	1,266	310	385	23	46	2,030
All juvenile court	1,426	215	805	58	116	2,620
Official	(567)	(81)	(294)	(21)	(46)	(1,009)
Unofficial	(859)	(134)	(511)	(37)	(70)	(1,611)
Age						
8–10	88	22	81	9	2	202
11–13	430	81	292	25	42	870
14–16	1,443	282	559	35	83	2,402
17	731	140	258	12	35	1,176
Parents in home*						
2	920	128	396	46	77	1,567
1	412	70	345	9	28	864
0	85	17	63	3	10	178
Unknown	9	0	1	0	1	11
Family income*						
$0– 2,500	72	15	124	2	4	217
$2,500– 5,000	437	72	290	9	44	852
$5,000–10,000	391	32	90	18	31	562
Over $10,000	36	2	3	2	0	43
Unknown†	490	94	298	27	37	946

154 :

Variable Factors	White	White-Spanish	Negro	Chinese	Other	Total
Type of offense						
Robbery	19	6	34	1	4	64
Assault	52	10	95	3	8	168
Burglary	172	24	90	6	16	308
Theft except auto	245	48	220	25	27	565
Auto theft	227	27	67	11	10	342
Sex offenses	41	6	18	2	6	73
Delinquent tendencies & curfew	1,592	347	508	28	65	2,540
All other	344	57	158	5	26	590

* Parents in home and income were recorded for juvenile-court cases only.
† See Appendix B for explanation of "Unknown" income category.

Table C-2: Female Delinquent Population (1960) by Variable Factors Studied

Variable Factors	White	White-Spanish	Negro	Chinese	Other	Total
All delinquents	397	70	251	8	36	762
Police dept. only	97	17	24	1	0	139
All juvenile court	300	53	227	7	36	623
Official	(106)	(17)	(65)	(2)	(13)	(203)
Unofficial	(194)	(36)	(162)	(5)	(23)	(420)
Age						
8–10	6	2	12	0	0	20
11–13	55	11	77	1	10	154
14–16	248	45	132	7	20	452
17	88	12	30	0	6	136
Parents in home*						
2	154	32	100	5	25	316
1	109	16	107	2	7	241
0	37	4	19	0	4	64
Unknown	0	1	1	0	0	2
Family income*						
$0– 2,500	28	7	50	0	5	90
$2,500– 5,000	103	17	55	1	10	186
$5,000–10,000	35	7	24	1	4	71
Over $10,000	3	0	0	0	0	3
Unknown†	131	22	98	5	17	273

Variable Factors	White	White-Spanish	Negro	Chinese	Other	Total
Type of offense						
Robbery	0	0	0	0	0	0
Assault	4	1	14	0	1	20
Burglary	0	0	4	0	0	4
Theft except auto	38	11	70	5	5	129
Auto theft	3	2	4	0	1	10
Sex offenses	26	5	23	0	3	57
Delinquent tendencies & curfew	297	47	119	2	25	490
All other	29	4	17	1	1	52

* Parents in home and income were recorded for juvenile-court cases only.
† See Appendix B for explanation of "Unknown" income category.

Table C-3: Male Juvenile Populations (1960) of Negro-White and Chinese-White Comparison Areas by Age

| | NEGRO-WHITE AREA | | CHINESE-WHITE AREA | |
Age	Negro	White	Chinese	White
8–10	1,825	1,494	473	136
11–13	1,483	1,376	430	155
14–16	1,058	1,140	270	148
17	280	342	64	48
Total	4,646	4,352	1,237	487

Table C-4: Distribution of Children Not Living with Both Parents, by Age Groups, Western Urban Areas of the United States (1960)

| | PERCENTAGE OF ALL CHILDREN IN EACH AGE GROUP | | PERCENTAGE OF EACH AGE GROUP NOT LIVING WITH BOTH PARENTS | |
Age Group	White	Nonwhite	White	Nonwhite
0–7	33.8	44.9	8.4	26.7
8–10	21.5	15.9	16.1	25.6
11–13	12.3	13.0	9.8	23.1
14–16	13.9	17.4	12.3	48.0
17	18.5	8.7	41.3	46.2
0–17			12.2	29.2

Table C-5: Population at Risk, 1964 and 1960* by Color, Sex, Age, and Area of City

	White				Nonwhite				Total
	MALE		FEMALE		MALE		FEMALE		
Area	5–13	14–19	5–13	14–19	5–13	14–19	5–13	14–19	
Western area	13,993 (14,182)	10,437 (8,291)	13,845 (13,978)	9,126 (8,802)	2,484 (1,822)	1,417 (770)	2,481 (1,335)	1,393 (788)	55,176 (50,470)
Eastern area	16,233 (17,235)	11,058 (9,722)	15,724 (16,658)	10,864 (10,994)	11,899 (10,929)	5,727 (3,853)	11,474 (10,522)	5,941 (4,128)	88,920 (84,041)
Total	30,226 (31,417)	21,495 (18,013)	29,569 (30,636)	19,990 (19,796)	14,383 (12,751)	7,144 (4,623)	13,955 (12,259)	7,333 (4,916)	144,095 (134,511)

* Figures for 1960 are in parentheses.

Table C-6: Delinquent Population (1964) by Color, Sex, Age, Type of Interaction, and Area of City

| | White | | | | Nonwhite | | | | Total |
| | MALE | | FEMALE | | MALE | | FEMALE | | |
Interactions	5–13	14–19	5–13	14–19	5–13	14–19	5–13	14–19	
Juvenile-court cases									
Western area	100	435	27	91	65	187	17	52	974
Eastern area	311	866	79	227	456	940	124	290	3,293
Nonresident	—	—	—	—	—	—	—	—	771
All cases									
Western area	171	978	35	140	90	277	25	66	1,782
Eastern area	485	1,813	100	343	578	1,429	152	360	5,260
Nonresident	—	—	—	—	—	—	—	—	1,153
Total, all cases	656	2,791	135	483	668	1,706	177	426	8,195

APPENDIX D:
AREA ANALYSIS

Table D-1: Socioeconomic Indices Used in Area Analysis

Index	Abbreviation	Definition
Prematurity	PREM	Premature births per 1,000 live births, 1959–1961
Income *High Income*	HINC	Families with annual income over $10,-000 per 1,000 families
Low Income	LOINC	Families with annual income under $3,000 per 1,000 families
Nuclear Family	NUCFAM	Persons under 18 living with both parents per 1,000 persons under 18
Unemployment	UNEMPL	Unemployed males in civilian labor force per 1,000 males in civilian labor force
Working Female	WRKFEM	Women in labor force per 1,000 women over 14 in population
Separation	SEP	Separated females per 1,000 separated or divorced females
Occupation	OCC	Employed males in white-collar positions per 1,000 employed males
Education	EDUC	Persons over 25 who completed 8 years or less of school per 1,000 persons over 25
Homeowner	OWNER	Owner-occupied housing units per 1,000 occupied housing units
Crowding	CROWD	Occupied housing units with more than 1 person per room per 1,000 occupied housing units
Housing	HOUS	Combined tracts: sound housing units per 1,000 housing units Single-race tracts, white: sound housing units that are vacant or white-occupied per 1,000 such housing units Single-race tracts, nonwhite: sound housing units that are nonwhite-occupied per 1,000 such housing units
Integration	INTEG	White population per 1,000 total population

Table D-2: Factor Analysis of Variables

	COMBINED DATA			SINGLE-RACE DATA (REFLECTED)		
Index	Factor I	Factor II	Factor III	Factor I	Factor II	Factor III
PREM	−.3576	−.1210	.6744	−.5307	.1710	.4422
HINC	.8994	.1834	−.1735	.8588	−.0961	.0798
LOINC	−.8087	−.3544	.2729	−.8126	−.0996	.0980
NUCFAM	.4407	.2312	−.6877	.6444	−.0056	−.6711
UNEMPL	−.8310	−.3445	.2245	−.8991	−.0549	.0336
WRKFEM	.0709	−.8371	−.1127	−.1367	−.7989	−.0349
SEP	−.7198	.0580	.4798	−.7964	.2094	.1592
OCC	.9267	−.1852	−.0407	.8561	−.0933	.0783
EDUC	−.8802	.0508	−.1721	−.7541	.1747	−.3997
OWNER	.4506	.6793	−.0518	.6821	.6607	.0434
CROWD	−.8924	−.0526	−.0420	−.7429	.1627	−.3517
HOUS	.7833	.1637	−.1792	.7984	−.0585	.0517
INTEG	.6002	.5101	−.0609	.7286	.2765	.2361

Table D-3: Prediction of Delinquency by Multiple Regression

	COMBINED DATA		SINGLE-RACE DATA	
	Male Delinquency	Female Delinquency	Male Delinquency	Female Delinquency
Constant	60.11	70.98	81.28	69.39
Coefficient, factor I	0.38	0.42	0.48	0.23
Coefficient, factor II	—	—	—	—
Coefficient, factor III	0.18	—	1.10	0.62
Multiple correlation coefficient	0.297	0.205	0.664	0.364
Percentage of variance of delinquency explained by regression	8.8%	4.2%	44.0%	13.2%

Table D-4: Predicted and Observed Mean Delinquency Rates by Sex and Race, Single-Race Data Analysis. For both male and female rates the Negro-White differences are significant

Race and Sex	Predicted	Observed
Chinese male	40.4	36.6
White male	50.3	49.4
Negro male	54.1	59.4
Chinese female	44.5	39.6
White female	50.2	48.3
Negro female	52.1	61.4

Selected Bibliography

A. SUPPLEMENTARY REFERENCES

No attempt has been made to cite all of the vast literature on juvenile delinquency and related subjects. Those who are interested in doing additional reading will find the following publications informative.

Cabot, P. S. de Q. *Juvenile Delinquency: A Critical Annotated Bibliography.* New York: H. W. Wilson, 1946. Reviews literature to 1944.

Chilman, Catherine S. *Growing Up Poor.* Welfare Administration Publication No. 13. Washington: Department of Health, Education, and Welfare, 1966. Reviews literature on the effects of poverty on children.

Miller, Elizabeth W. *The Negro in America: A Bibliography.* Cambridge, Mass.: Harvard University Press, 1966.

National Clearinghouse for Mental Health Information. *Crime and Delinquency Abstracts.* Bethesda, Md.: National Institute of Mental Health. Continues former publication, *International Bibliography on Crime and Delinquency,* and includes current research projects.

Spector, H. K. *Juvenile Delinquency: A Bibliography.* San Quentin, Calif.: California State Prison, n.d. (ca. 1963). A selective bibliography to 1961.

Tompkins, Dorothy C. *Juvenile Gangs and Street Groups: A Bibliography.* Berkeley: University of California Institute of Governmental Studies, 1966.

Welsch, E. K. *The Negro in the United States: A Research Guide.* Bloomington: Indiana University Press, 1965. Annotated bibliography to 1964.

B. REFERENCES CITED IN TEXT

Abrahams, R. *Deep Down in the Jungle.* Hatboro, Pa., Folklore Associates, 1964.

Adamson, L., and H. W. Dunham. "Clinical Treatment of Male Delinquents: A Case Study in Effort and Result," *Am. Sociol. Rev.,* 21: (June 1956), 312–320.

Akers, R. L. "Socioeconomic Status and Delinquent Behavior—A Retest," *J. Res. in Crime and Del.,* 1: (January 1964), 38–46.

Amos, W. E. "Prevention Through the School," in W. E. Amos and C. F. Wellford (eds.), *Delinquency Prevention: Theory and Practice.* Englewood Cliffs, N.J.: Prentice-Hall, 1967, Ch. 7.

———, **R. L. Manella, and M. A. Southwell.** *Action Programs for Delinquency Prevention.* Springfield, Ill.: Charles C. Thomas, 1965.

Ariès, P. *Centuries of Childhood: A Social History of Family Life,* trans. R. Baldick. New York: Vintage Books, 1965.

Bell, R. R. "The One Parent Mother in the Negro Lower Class." Paper read at Eastern Sociological Meetings. New York, April, 1965. Philadelphia: Sociology Department, Temple University, 1965.

Bernstein, S. *Youth on the Streets.* New York: Association Press, 1964.

Bingley, T. *Mental Symptoms in Temporal Lobe Epilepsy and Temporal Lobe Gliomas.* København: Ejnar Munksgaard, 1958.

Blauner, R. "Whitewash over Watts," *Trans-Action,* 3: (March-April 1966), 3–9, 54.

Blumer, H., A. Sutter, R. Smith, and S. Ahmed. *The World of Youthful Drug Use.* Berkeley: University of California School of Criminology, 1967.

Bogue, D. J., and Beverly Duncan. Vital Stat. Spec. Rep. 47: No. 6. *A Composite Method for Estimating Postcensal Population of Small Areas by Age, Sex and Color.* Washington: Department of Health, Education, and Welfare, (August 24, 1959).

Bordua, D. J. "Juvenile Delinquency and 'Anomie': An Attempt at Replication," *Social Problems,* 6: (Winter 1959), 230–238.

———. *Sociological Theories and Their Implications for Juvenile Delinquency.* Washington: U.S. Children's Bureau, 1960.

Bowlby, J. *Maternal Care and Mental Health.* Geneva: World Health Organization, 1952.
Brown, C. *Manchild in the Promised Land.* New York: Macmillan, 1965.
Bruyn, H. B., and R. H. Seiden. "Student Suicide: Fact or Fancy," *J. Am. College Health Assn.,* 14 (December 1965), 69–77.
California Youth Authority. *The Community Treatment Project After 5 Years.* Department of the Youth Authority, n.d. (ca.1967).
Caesar, G. "Scandal In the Job Corps," *True,* 47: (December 1966), 33–35, 64, 70, 73.
Chaitin, M. R., and H. W. Dunham. "The Juvenile Court in its Relationship to Adult Criminology: A Replicated Study," *Social Forces,* 45 (September 1966), 114–119.
Chilton, R. J. "Continuity in Delinquency Area Research: A Comparison of Studies for Baltimore, Detroit, and Indianapolis," *Am. Sociol. Rev.,* 29 (1964), 71–83.
Cloward, R., and L. Ohlin. *Delinquency and Opportunity.* New York: Free Press, 1960.
Coles, R. "Violence in Ghetto Children," *Children,* 14: (May–June 1967), 101–104.
Craig, Maude M., and P. W. Furst. "What Happens After Treatment? A Study of Potentially Delinquent Boys," *Soc. Serv. Rev.,* 39 (June 1965), 165–171.
———, **and Selma J. Glick.** "Ten Years Experience with the Glueck Social Prediction Table," *Crime and Delinquency,* 9: (July 1963), 249–261.
Drake, St. C. "The Social and Economic Status of the Negro in the United States," *Daedalus,* 94 (Winter 1965), 771–814.
Earle, K. M., M. Baldwin, and W. Penfield. "Incisural Sclerosis and Temporal Lobe Seizures Produced by Hippocampal Herniation at Birth," *AMA Arch. Neur. Psych.,* 69 (January 1953), 27–42.
Eaton, J. W., and K. Polk. *Measuring Juvenile Delinquency. A Study of Probation Department Referrals.* Pittsburgh: University of Pittsburgh Press, 1961.
Eisner, V. "Effect of Parents in Home on Juvenile Delinquency," *Pub. Health Rep.,* 81 (October 1966), 905–910.
———. "Reported Juvenile Delinquency in San Francisco, 1960–65," *Pub. Health Rep.,* 82 (February 1967), 163–168.
———, **and H. Tsuyemura.** "Interactions of Juveniles with the Law," *Pub. Health Rep.,* 80 (August 1965), 681–691.
Erikson, E. H. *Childhood and Society.* 2d ed. New York: Norton, 1963.

————, and **K. T. Erikson.** "Confirmation of the Delinquent." Chicago Rev. (Winter 1957).

Erikson, K. T. "Notes on the Sociology of Deviance," in H. S. Becker (ed.), *The Other Side: Perspectives on Deviance.* New York: Free Press, 1964, pp. 9–21.

Frazier, E. F. *The Negro Family in the United States.* Rev. ed. New York: Citadel Press, 1948.

Friedenberg, E. Z. *Coming of Age in America.* New York: Random House, 1963.

Glaser, K., and R. L. Clemmens. "School Failure," *Ped.,* 35 (January 1965), 128–141.

Glueck, S., and E. Glueck. *Unraveling Juvenile Delinquency.* New York: Commonwealth Fund, 1950.

————. *Family Environment and Delinquency.* Boston: Houghton Mifflin, 1962.

Gordon, M. "Five Signs on the Highroad," *Saturday Review,* April 6, 1963, pp. 49–52.

Gordon, S. "The Brain-Injured Adolescent," *Child and Family,* 5 (Spring 1966), 53–60.

Hansen, E., M. Forrester, and F. Bird. *The Tenderloin Ghetto: The Young Reject in our Society.* San Francisco: Glide Urban Center, n.d. (ca.1966).

Hathaway, S. R., and E. D. Monachesi. *Adolescent Personality and Behavior.* Minneapolis: University of Minnesota Press, 1963.

Healy, W., and Augusta F. Bronner. *New Light on Delinquency and its Treatment.* New Haven: Yale University Press, 1936.

Hill, M. "The Metropolis and Juvenile Delinquency Among Negroes," *J. Negro Educ.,* 28 (Summer 1959), 277–285.

Jacobs, Jane. *The Death and Life of Great American Cities.* New York: Random House, 1961.

Johnson, Adelaide. "Causation of Juvenile Delinquency," *Ped.,* 17 (June 1956), 934–939.

Keil, Charles. *Urban Blues.* Chicago: University of Chicago Press, 1966.

King, M. L., Jr. *Where Do We Go From Here: Chaos or Community?* New York: Harper & Row, 1967.

Krueger, G. M. *Survey of Probation Officers, 1959.* Washington: Department of Health, Education, and Welfare, 1960.

Kvaraceus, W. C. "Forecasting Delinquency: A Three Year Experiment," *Exceptional Children,* 27 (April 1961), 429–435.

————, **W. B. Miller,** *et al. Delinquent Behavior, Culture and the Individual.* Washington: National Education Association of the United States, 1959.

Lander, B. *Towards an Understanding of Juvenile Delinquency.* New York: Columbia University Press, 1954.

Lentz, W. P. "Delinquency as a Stable Role," *Soc. Work,* 11 (October 1966), 66–70.

Lewis, O. *La Vida, A Puerto Rican Family in the Culture of Poverty—San Juan and New York.* New York: Random House, 1966.

Lilienfeld, A. M., and B. Pasamanick. "Association of Maternal and Fetal Factors With the Development of Epilepsy," *J. Am. Med. Ass.,* 155 (June 19, 1954), 719–724.

Lin Tsung-yi. "Two Types of Delinquent Youth in Chinese Society," in M. K. Oppler (ed.), *Culture and Mental Health.* New York: Macmillan, 1959, pp. 257–271.

Lippitt, Peggy, and J. E. Lohman. "Cross-Age Relationships—An Educational Resource," *Children,* 12 (May–June 1965), 113–117.

Lohman, J. D. *Juvenile Delinquency: Its Dimensions, Its Conditions, Techniques of Control, Proposals for Action.* Office of the Sheriff, Cook County, Illinois, 1957.

———, **and R. M. Carter.** "The Adolescent Social System in Relation to Middle Class Delinquency." Paper read to Am. Orthopsych. Assn., San Francisco, April 13–16, 1966. Berkeley: University of California School of Criminology, 1966.

Long, H. H. "No Hiding Place: The Negro Search," in D. Schrieber (ed.), *The School Dropout.* Washington: National Education Association, 1964, pp. 75–88.

Loomis, S. D. "EEG Abnormalities as a Correlate of Behavior in Adolescent Male Delinquents," *Am. J. Psych.,* 121 (April 1965), 1003–1006.

Low, N. L., and S. P. Dawson. "Electroencephalographic Findings in Juvenile Delinquency," *Ped.,* 28 (September 1961), 452–457.

Lucas, A. R., E. A. Rodin, and C. B. Simson. "Neurological Assessment of Children with Early School Problems," *Devel. Med. Child Neurol.,* 7 (April 1965), 145–156.

MacDonald, Mary E. "Verdict Before Trial: A Review of the Test by the New York City Youth Board of the Glueck Social Prediction Table," *Soc. Serv. Rev.,* 39 (June 1965), 172–182.

MacIver, R. M. *The Prevention and Control of Delinquency.* New York: Atherton Press, 1966.

Matza, D. *Delinquency and Drift.* New York: Wiley, 1964.

McNassor, D. "This Frantic Pace in Education," *J. Secondary Educ.,* 42 (March 1967), 99–105.

Merwin, D. J. (ed.). *Reaching the Fighting Gang.* New York: New York City Youth Board, 1960.

Miller, W. B. "Implications of Urban Lower Class Culture for Social Work," *Soc. Serv. Rev.,* 33 (September 1959), 219–236.

————, **H. Geertz, and H. S. G. Cutter.** "Aggression in a Boys' Streetcorner Group," *Psychiatry,* 24 (November 1961), 283–298.

National Advisory Commission on Civil Disorders. Report. New York, Bantam, 1968.

Nye, F. I., J. F. Short, and V. J. Olsen. "Socioeconomic Status and Delinquent Behavior," *Am. J. Sociol.,* 63 (January 1958), 381–389.

Oppenheimer, E., and M. Mendel. "Behavior Disturbances of School Children in Relation to the Preschool Period," *Am. J. Public Health,* 49 (November 1959), 1537–1542.

Pearl, A., and Frank Riessman. *New Careers for the Poor.* New York: Free Press, 1965.

Perlman, I. R. "Juvenile Delinquency and Some Social and Economic Trends," *Welfare in Rev.,* 1 (October 1963), 12–21.

Piliavin, I., and S. Briar. "Police Encounters with Juveniles," *Am. J. Sociol.,* 70 (September 1964), 206–214.

————, **and C. Werthman.** "Gang Members and the Police," in D. Bordua (ed.), *The Police.* New York: Wiley, 1967, pp. 59–98.

Purcel, F. P. *Low Income Youth, Unemployment, Vocational Training, and the Job Corps.* New York: Center for Study of Unemployed Youth, New York University, 1966.

Rainwater, L. "Crucible of Identity: The Negro Lower-Class Family," *Daedalus,* 95 (Winter 1966), 172–216.

Redl, F., and D. Wineman. *Children Who Hate.* New York: Free Press, 1951.

Reiss, A. J., and A. L. Rhodes. "The Distribution of Juvenile Delinquency in the Social Class Structure," *Am. Sociol. Rev.,* 26 (October 1961), 720–732.

Rice, R. E., and S. Adams. *The Correctional Costs of Serviced and Unserviced Juvenile Gangs.* Research Office Report No. 23. Los Angeles: County Probational Department, 1965.

Rubenfeld, S. *Family of Outcasts: A New Theory of Delinquency.* New York: Free Press, 1965.

San Francisco Juvenile Court. Annual Report. San Francisco: Youth Guidance Center, 1960, 1964.

Shaffer, T. E. "The Zone Between Social Acceptance and Juvenile Delinquency," *J. Ped.,* 59 (November 1961), 747–751.

Shaw, C., and H. D. McKay. *Juvenile Delinquency in Urban Areas.* Chicago: University of Chicago Press, 1942.

Snow, John. *On the Mode of Communication of Cholera.* London: John Churchill, 1855; reprinted New York: Commonwealth Fund, 1936.

Spergel, I. *Street Gang Work: Theory and Practice.* Reading, Mass.: Addison Wesley, 1966.

Stapleton, T. "Pediatrics, Psychiatry, and Delinquency," *J. Ped.,* 60 (May 1962), 740–745.

Stetler, H. G. *Comparative Study of Negro and White Dropouts in Selected Connecticut High Schools.* Hartford, Conn.: Commission on Civil Rights, 1959.

Tappan, P. W. "Who Is the Criminal?" *Am. Soc. Rev.,* 12 (February 1947), 96–102.

Tryon, R. C., and D. E. Bailey. "The BC IRY Computer System of Cluster and Factor Analysis," *Multivariate Behav. Res.,* 1 (January 1966), 95–111.

Tunley, R. *Kids, Crime and Chaos: A World Report on Juvenile Delinquency.* New York: Harper & Row, 1962.

U.S. Bureau of the Census. *U.S. Census of Population and Housing: 1960.* Census Tracts. Final Report PHC (1)–137. Washington: Government Printing Office, 1962.

U.S. Children's Bureau. *Health Services and Juvenile Delinquency.* Children's Bureau Publ. No. 353. Washington: Department of Health, Education, and Welfare, 1955.

U.S. Children's Bureau. *A Look at Juvenile Delinquency.* Children's Bureau Publication No. 380. Washington: Department of Health, Education, and Welfare, 1960, p. 38.

U.S. Children's Bureau. *Juvenile Court Statistics–1965.* Stat. Series No. 85. Washington: Department of Health, Education, and Welfare, 1966.

U.S. Dept. of Labor, *The Negro Family: The Case for National Action.* Washington: Office of Policy Planning and Research, U.S. Department of Labor, 1965.

Werthman, C. "Delinquents in Schools: A Test for the Legitimacy of Authority," *Berkeley J. of Sociol.,* 8 (1963), 39–60.

Williamson, H., and R. L. Keiser. *Hustler.* New York: Doubleday, 1965.

Witmer, Helen L. *Delinquency and the Adolescent Crisis.* Children's Bureau, Washington: Department of Health, Education, and Welfare, 1960.

———, **and Edith Tufts.** *The Effectiveness of Delinquency Prevention Programs.* Children's Bureau Publication No. 340. Washington: Department of Health, Education, and Welfare, 1954.

Index